Getting Started in

FOREX TRADING STRATEGIES

The *Getting Started In* Series

Getting Started in

FOREX TRADING STRATEGIES

SEVENTH EDITION

Michael Duane Archer

BICENTENNIAL
1807
WILEY
2007
BICENTENNIAL

John Wiley & Sons, Inc.

Published by John Wiley & Sons, Inc., Hoboken, New Jersey.
Published simultaneously in Canada.

Wiley Bicentennial Logo: Richard J. Pacifico.

For general information on our other products and services or for technical support, please contact our Customer Care Department within the United States at (800) 762-2974, outside the United States at (317) 572-3993 or fax (317) 572-4002.

Wiley also publishes its books in a variety of electronic formats. Some content that appears in print may not be available in electronic formats. For more information about Wiley products, visit our Web site at www.wiley.com.

Library of Congress Cataloging-in-Publication Data:

Archer, Michael D. (Michael Duane)
    Getting started in Forex trading strategies / Michael D. Archer.
        p. cm. — (The getting started in series)
ISBN 978-0-470-07392-6 (pbk.)
1. Foreign exchange market. 2. Foreign exchange futures. 3. Speculation. I. Title.
HG3851.A7392 2007
332.4'5—dc22

2007023236

Printed in the United States of America

10 9 8 7 6 5 4 3 2 1

To My Wife, Elaine

Contents

Getting Started in

FOREX TRADING STRATEGIES

Introduction

Do something different, even if it's wrong.

—Charles B. Goodman

Getting Started in FOREX Trading Strategies

Getting Started in FOREX Trading Strategies is intended as a sequel to *Getting Started in Currency Trading (GSICT)*, although it may certainly be used independently. One comment readers often make after reading the latter is, "Great, now I know the mechanics of FOREX. But what do I do next?" This book addresses that question. However, it does assume some basic knowledge of FOREX.

If you are new to currency trading, I suggest you pick up a copy of *Getting Started in Currency Trading* and read and study the material before starting this volume.

Readers' expectations vary enormously. Most thought "getting started" truly meant getting started, but some assumed the book would carry them through more advanced training. A few were disappointed not to find a $19.95 black-box system leading to great wealth without effort. There is no get-rich-quick method in FOREX or any other market. *Getting Started in FOREX Trading Strategies (GSIFTS)* is meant to give you an initial perspective on various methods and a simple method on which to build.

Traditional Strategies

To most traders, *strategy* is synonymous with *trading techniques*—one or more of the many flavors of price charts or indicators such as oscillators and moving averages. In *GSIFTS*, strategy refers to the three primary elements that define a trader: trading techniques, money management, and the soft elements of market selection, trader profile, tactics, and psychology. Together they compose a trader's style.

1

A traditional trading strategy includes a charting technique such as point and figure or candlestick charts, a number of technical indicators, and perhaps a few other tools the trader has found useful in previous trading. Money management is typically an ad hoc set of rules for limiting losses, maximizing gains, and entering and exiting a trade. Most traditional strategies rarely consider style, or soft elements, in any depth.

Traditional strategies represent a linear approach to trading. Each strategic element is separate from the other. The elements don't communicate very well, if at all, with each other. The codex approach, introduced herein, applies a process paradigm to the elements and to trading.

Trading Strategies: The Elements

- Trading tools ("toolbox")
- Money management
- Soft elements
  - Style
  - Psychology and attitude

There is nothing inherently wrong with traditional strategies and the elements approach. Some traders are very successful with them. A plethora of print and online material currently exists for the traditional trader. But let's look at the facts. The FOREX market is not unlike other highly leveraged markets, such as options or futures. The statistics are not pretty; nearly 90 percent of new traders lose their initial account deposit in less than six months—most of them using traditional strategies.

I recently attended a FOREX convention in Las Vegas. I observed someone lecturing on chart support and resistance points. Useful information, to be sure, but probably not in the way the lecturer intended. The vast majority of traditional currency traders will be looking for the same or nearly the same support and resistance points. The market *never* cooperates with the majority; if it did, everyone would be a winner and it would soon cease to exist. To the codex trader, the traditional support and resistance points are useful only to see what other traders are thinking. The codex trader will seek to find the market's true stopping and turning points.

The Codex Process

The codex approach introduced in *Getting Started in FOREX Trading Strategies* attempts to meld the three elements into a trading process. Changes to one element, such as trading technique, will reverberate to the other elements. Instead of looking at the elements individually, a personal trading codex folds them into a process beginning with finding good trading candidates and concluding with a short postmortem of each completed trade.

An analysis of each completed trade allows the trader to adjust his trading codex in an evolutionary, rather than revolutionary, manner. The specific codex method I use is named FxCodex in this book. *Codex* refers generally to the process method of trading; *FxCodex* refers to the specific elements I use to trade currencies as a process.

Trading Strategies: Codex

- Tracking
- Selecting
- Entry
- Monitoring
- Exit

Steps to Strategic Success

A codex is very personal and will differ with each trader. The FxCodex method is my personal way of trading. *GSIFTS* will use it to explore the codex philosophy but offer individual choices for traders who want to go in a different direction. The key is developing a trading codex leading to a *process* rather than an *elements* trading approach.

Principles of Codex and FxCodex

- Codex is a process.
- Each step in a process is based on previous steps.
- Steps talk to each other.
- A change in one step of the process requires other steps to be adjusted.
- Process changes should be evolutionary rather than revolutionary.
- *FxCodex* is the name given my specific codex.

Developing any personal trading codex requires the trader to make a number of initial decisions. These decisions will define your initial trading codex. You can begin with a simple, basic structure and add to it as your experiences in the market dictate. This is just one of the advantages of the codex approach.

These decision *steps* are the transition required to move from a traditional-elements approach to a codex-process approach to trading. Too many traders begin without having made these decisions and then make sharp revolutionary changes in strategies as they go along. It is far better to have a codex defined before making any trades and make small, evolutionary adjustments thereafter.

The traditional strategies give heavy emphasis to trading tools, often ignoring money management and soft elements such as style, market selection, psychology, and tactics. The codex approach gives equal emphasis to all of them and places them in a process paradigm. See Figure I.1.

The trader may move back and forth between these steps before having fully built a codex. You may find, for example, that you have selected currency pairs inappropriate for your trading style. If so, you may want to go back and consider the selection of currency pairs vis-à-vis that information. The codex approach allows you to weave back and forth without major disruption to your overall trading method.

Tools

Your first step is to decide the trading tools or techniques you will use. The number of technical analysis tools is legend. There are dozens of charting techniques, indicators by the hundreds, and a myriad of methods, systems, techniques, and black boxes. It would be neither practical nor possible to assign all of them to the codex tool box.

In my opinion (after 30 years in the markets), systems and black boxes don't work consistently over different market environments and for long periods of time. If you find one that does, call me. Making money in the markets requires real work and constant diligence.

The most important factors in selecting codex tools are *transparency* and *simplicity*. If you cannot understand how a tool works and what it really does,

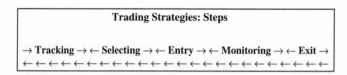

FIGURE I.1　Trading Strategies: Steps.

don't use it. Making evolutionary adjustments to your codex requires you to be able to understand the tools you use for trading.

The trading technique backbone of the FxCodex method is charting. Most charts are simple, transparent, and visual. You can *see* what they mean. Indicators are often opaque; what are they really measuring? If you don't know what a tool does, how can you make adjustments when things go bad?

If you carefully examine many of the indicators available—typically a type of moving average or oscillator—you will discover the following: (1) The indicators are curve-fit to a specific market environment, and (2) they are really only variations of the slope-intercept formula you learned in eighth-grade algebra. They measure the slope of the price changes in a market. You can see that better and faster by simply eyeballing a chart.

Which charting technique should you use for your codex? Bar charts? Point and figure charts? Candlesticks? Swing charts? In fact, any will work just fine! Whatever charting tool you are most comfortable with, use it. I use bar charts primarily for finding trade candidates and then switch to swing charts for market entry and exit. This book gives examples using all of them.

Of course, you must interpret whatever charts you select. Traditional traders use such methods as support and resistance levels. They can be effective, but too many people are using them for the market to cooperate, in my opinion. How can all these traders be successful? In fact, we know they are not and cannot be. Don't be afraid to be in the minority; only a minority of traders is ever successful.

Charles B. Goodman was a commodities grain trader from Eads, Colorado. He became my mentor shortly after I began trading in 1973. Charlie entrusted to me many of his trading methods, the most significant of which I have introduced in this book as the Goodman Swing Count System, the Goodman Cycle Count System, and Market Environments. Perhaps even more useful was his astute money management approach to trading, which I have also shared with the reader.

The Goodman Swing Count System (GSCS) has stood me well for my entire trading career spanning more than 30 years. It's an excellent way to get a quick fix on any market and for determining entry and exit points. It's a good method for beginners or near beginners. You may use it effectively right away to trade and then plumb its more advanced features as your comfort level and trading experience increase. Such things as support and resistance will usually not be in the same places as they are using traditional chart interpretation concepts.

I rely on GSCS heavily in this book. It is the cornerstone of the FxCodex method. Remember, the FxCodex method is used primarily to show you how to develop and apply your own personal trading codex. What works for me may not work for you. The important idea is to develop a comprehensive and consistent codex for trading.

I have never been a fan of technical indicators. It is difficult to see what they actually do, or measure. Most of them require a curve-fit to some specific market environment, and when the environment changes, the indicator flops. Moving averages work well in trending markets but fall apart in trading markets. Oscillators work great in trading markets but fail in trending markets. Nonetheless I've included two that are simpler, that provide information not easily visible with any chart, and that can be adjusted to different codex trading builds.

Market filters, typically statistical, are easy to implement and they provide great value for all traders. Strategy may find you the pot of gold, but it is often tactics that allow you to bring it home. Filters assist you in deciding what markets to avoid and on what markets to focus your valuable and limited time. Most of the market filters detailed in this book derive from the *FOREX Companion* series of books, written by this author and James Bickford.

Markets

Your second step is to select which currency pairs and crosses you want to at least begin trading. You may want to add or subtract pairs as you go along, but such swaps should be facilitated in an evolutionary, not revolutionary, fashion. This book lists five pairs and five crosses to meet a wide range of trading interests and propensities. The codex method allows you to keep more pairs and crosses on a monitor status and easily bring them into your trading if certain criteria are met.

The most popular markets are those including either the euro (EUR) or the U.S. dollar (USD). Five of the seven markets include one or both of these. The so-called *exotics* may offer exceptional opportunity, but they also command exceptional risk.

Currency pairs have different personalities and generally evolve slowly. The trader wants very much to select pairs for which his codex is a good fit. If you have an aggressive trading codex, select high-volatility pairs. If you are a very conservative trader, select low-volatility pairs. There are several other currency selection criteria that I discuss in *GSIFTS*.

Money Management and the Soft Elements

Your third step is to define yourself as a trader. This is a critical step and one most traders accomplish only by default. You will save a great deal of time and avoid much frustration by working through this process as early as possible in your trading career. Too many traders overemphasize the specific tools needed for trading and fail to apply the "know thyself" rule as traders.

What markets do you like to trade? Probably the ones in which you enjoy the greatest success. Analyze those for the characteristics that make them work, and stick to markets with those characteristics.

What are your personality traits as they relate to trading? Are you a calm or nervous sort of person, for example? Are you conservative or aggressive? What are your financial means and goals? Will you be trading an account of $3,000 or $30,000? How much are you really comfortable risking *in toto* and on any specific trade?

What money management ideas are best for you and for the tools in your codex? Are your selections realistic, and do they complement each other? Money management is *not* about how much money you can make. It's about avoiding losses. If you stay in the game long enough, you *will* make money. But if you lose your grubstake, you will not be in the game for that big payoff day.

My mentor, Charles B. Goodman, emphasized this over and over to me. I call it the *Belgian Dentist* approach. In Europe, Belgian dentists are considered the most conservative of traders. Trade the long term to break even; always consider risk above reward. I know, that doesn't sound very sexy. But if you break even over and over again, you will eventually win.

The primary money management parameters for all traders are the following:

- Aggregate account drawdown or risk.
- Win-to-loss percentage for specific trades.
- Aggregate percentage of wins to losses.

Different traders will modulate these parameters in different proportions, but it is important to set your standards up front, be realistic about them, and confirm that they are in agreement with the rest of your codex.

Getting Started in FOREX Trading Strategies—Sections in Summary

The following summary outlines the sections that make up *GSIFTS*.

Traditional Elements of FOREX Strategy

This comprises a brief overview of the traditional elements—trading techniques, money management, and style. A basic knowledge of the elements is important to the topic of developing the codex. The brief discussions are intended to get you thinking about your own personal likes, dislikes, successes, failures, and propensities as a trader.

Developing a Trading Codex

This section describes the important transition from traditional element strategies to the process codex strategy. The reader should spend as much time here as possible, taking pen to paper and pouring out his own thoughts on every aspect of trading.

The FxCodex Method

FxCodex is my personal codex. It is used in *Getting Started in FOREX Trading Strategies* to show you how to implement a codex of your own.

The key to the FxCodex approach is transparency. As a trader, you will gradually zero in on high-percentage opportunities using simple and understandable trading techniques. You will apply consistent money management rules consistent with your trading style and the soft elements.

No matter how good a trader you are, things do not always go as planned. The FxCodex method allows for on-the-fly diagnostics. Traditional traders too often redefine themselves and their strategies when things go awry. This is not good; evolution is more effective than revolution. Do your codex due diligence before you risk a dime in the markets.

This section also offers the reader some alternative codex selections for those who want to go their own way. Several trading campaigns hopefully bring home the codex approach to trading and its differences from traditional strategies.

The Complete FOREX Trader

The successful trader never ceases to explore and evolve! But the key is to make changes in harmony with your codex in an evolutionary rather than revolutionary manner. Record keeping is a vital resource for such activities. Written accounts of your trades and daily and weekly summaries not only allow you to accurately monitor your progress but also provide a feedback loop for improvements and codex quality control.

The Layout of *GSIFTS*

A final note about the layout of *GSIFTS*: This book is highly visual. Text is kept to a minimum and much information is provided in the charts, diagrams, tables, and explanations. Boxes provide a different perspective on especially difficult or important concepts, or provide ideas for independent study. I am a big fan of the visual approach to both studying and trading FOREX.

Building Blocks

The book attempts a building-block approach to developing the codex method. Part 1 introduces the elements, Part 2 details them in the context of the codex approach, and Part Three shows them in application. The same information may appear to be repeated, but the context is important and the repetition is useful to fully mastering the ideas.

As a writer and a trader I am always interested in comments, suggestions, and questions. No matter the vast reservoir of information available to us, we each can see the trading world only through our own eyes. Sometimes the view from another perspective can be enlightening. You may write to me at Duane@FxPraxis.com.

If you would like to keep abreast of the codex trading approach in general and the FxCodex method in particular, please visit www.fxpraxis.com.

Good trading!

Acknowledgments

A special thank you to Intellicharts for the use of their outstanding FOREX charts from their online service, FxTrek, www.fxtrek.com; and to Dawn Borris for her many suggestions, editing assistance and moral support.

Part

1

Traditional Elements of FOREX Strategy

Chapter 1

Trading Techniques

There are enough ideas for beating the markets to make you very rich—or very poor.

—Charles B. Goodman

Most traders consider trading techniques—the actual tools they use to make trading decisions—as the most important element of trading. The proof is in the pudding; just consider the corpus of information both in print and online that deals with trading techniques. The sheer amount is staggering.

As the FOREX market matures, some literature on money management and the soft elements is becoming available, but it is still dwarfed by information available about trading techniques. The demand continues to be for information on trading techniques. That is unfortunate given the importance of the other two elements.

Systems and Black Boxes

Before considering some of the most popular trading techniques or tools, let me briefly discuss systems and black boxes.

A *system* is a self-contained way to make trades. Systems generate specific buy and sell signals. Many FOREX trading systems are available either from broker/dealers or from third-party vendors. They are intended to be complete in and of themselves, although many traders still use them in conjunction with other trading techniques.

Systems typically show outstanding results over historic data, or they would not sell. But the historic data is very often curve fit. This means that the system was developed to fit the data and not the other way around. If that data related to some specific types of markets, such as volatile markets, trading markets, or trending markets, when the music changes the system is bound to fail.

Systems have always been popular in all the markets—stocks, options, futures, and now FOREX. Not all systems are bad, but they are all opaque and that is always a warning sign. See Figure 1.1.

Opaque and Transparent

If a trading tool is *opaque*, it is difficult or impossible to fully analyze what it measures. If a trading tool is *transparent*, what it measures is either obvious or easy to comprehend.

Indicators are generally opaque. *Charts* are transparent.

If you insist on using a system in your trading, be sure you understand which type of market it was build for or around—and use it only in those markets. However, determining which type of market the system was built for can be difficult. Many systems provide limited information regarding how they were developed. The best process is to look at charts of the markets vis-à-vis the system's performance. In which markets did it perform best—trading, trending, fast, slow? If the system vendor does not provide at least enough information to do this analysis, beware.

Black boxes are systems for which no information is available. You don't know how they were built, how they work, or what type of data they were built around. My recommendation regarding black box systems is to stay away from them. The less transparent the tool, the more difficult it is to make adjustments when things go wrong. A black box is the most opaque tool of all.

Robots have become popular in the FOREX markets. Usually, these are programs that automatically execute a trading system. In fast-moving markets they are very useful, especially to the professional money manager overseeing dozens or even hundreds of separate accounts. If your available time for trading is limited, you may want to consider using robots.

But if you have so little time to trade that a robot appeals to you, I recommend that you consider a professional money manager to trade your account. There are many money managers with excellent track records, but a discussion is beyond the scope of this book. Seek out a manager who has

FIGURE 1.1 Curve-Fit Data.

The moving average is curve-fit to the data. A five-day average was selected on previous market performance. There is no guarantee that the future market performance will work with this value.

Source: FXtrek Intellichart™. Copyright 2001–2007 FXtrek.com, Inc.

performed well in a variety of markets. It is more important that the manager has done well in a spectrum of market types than in specific pairs or crosses.

Technical versus Fundamental Analysis

Most traders today use technical analysis to trade. This refers to techniques based on price and other objective data that result from market action. The technician's credo is "Everything is in the market price."

The factors examined in fundamental analysis, such as a country's income, gross national product, and interest rates certainly drive currency prices in the long run. The problem for the currency trader is, as Keynes said, "In the long run we are all dead." The FOREX markets are highly leveraged; this is one of their main attractions. You can be correct about a currency pair in the long run, but the leverage may cause a price movement more than ample in degree to take you out of the market before you can profit from being correct about the fundamentals. It is discouraging to be correct in your determination of long-term trend direction—for example, "Interest rates will drive the U.S. dollar lower against the euro"—but lose money because volatility and leverage cause so many short-term fluctuations that you are never able to board the long-term trend successfully.

No one denies that fundamentals such as money supply, labor statistics, political events, and many others drive the currency markets. The problem—and why most traders use technical analysis—is how to interpret them, especially in the short term.

Most fundamental information is quantitative but much is not. For example, how does a trader convert an unemployment statistic to a price value? To further complicate matters, there are hundreds of fundamentals that impact prices, and the matrix of possibilities is astronomical. And some fundamentals, such as geopolitical events, are not even quantifiable.

The prices in Figure 1.2—tracked hourly for 30 days on EUR/USD—were ultimately driven by a wide range of fundamentals. But how does the trader discern them in advance?

Technical analysis allows you to zoom in as close to the markets as you want. In fact, an advantage of technical analysis is the ability to visualize the markets at multiple price levels simultaneously. See Figures 1.3 through 1.5.

There is no perfect world, of course. Fundamentalists will counter that the prices you use to do technical analysis are already history by the time you do your calculations, and they have no rational effect on the future prices.

But a simple example will show this concept to be incorrect, at least in theory. It is true that after I enter my order to buy or sell, I have had all the

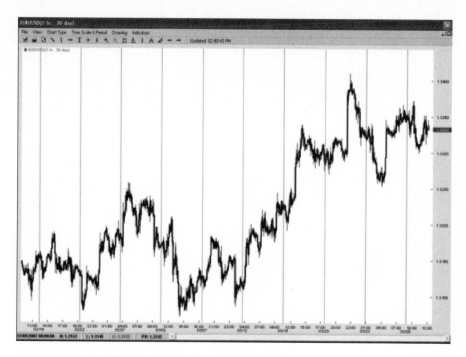

FIGURE 1.2 Fundamentals—Right and Still Wrong.
Source: FXtrekIntelliChart™. Copyright FXtrek.com, Inc.

impact on prices that I will have until I enter the opposite order to exit the market. Yet every trader has a propensity to exit the market, once entered, on variable factors of price and time. At what price will I take a profit? At what price will I take a loss? How long am I willing to stay in a trade? These propensities vary from trader to trader, but the aggregate of all propensities creates a push and pull on the market that should, again in theory, be measurable. See Table 1.1.

All traders have access to market prices; the same cannot be said of fundamentals. There are literally millions of fundamental factors in any given currency, and the relationships among them are in the billions. Someone will almost certainly know a piece of fundamental information before you do. And how do you translate a fundamental like gross domestic product (GDP) to a specific market value or even a specific entry price? To add gasoline to the fire, remember that these relationships are almost certainly nonlinear and are changing rapidly all the time.

Fundamental traders conclude that prices have no memory and that only raw fundamental information drives the markets. The following is only a partial list of potential fundamentals for the U.S. dollar (USD). Other countries will have similar lists. Now, don't you really want to be a technical trader!

FIGURE 1.3 Price Level Analysis: 15-Minute Bar Chart.
Source: FXtrek IntelliChart™. Copyright 2001–2007 FXtrek.com, Inc.

- ABC/*Money* magazine Consumer Comfort Index.
- Aggregate hours worked.
- Atlanta Fed index.
- Average hourly earnings.

FIGURE 1.4 Price Level Analysis: Hourly Bar Chart.
Source: FXtrek IntelliChart™. Copyright 2001–2007 FXtrek.com, Inc.

- Average weekly earnings.
- Average workweek.
- Balance of trade.
- Federal Reserve Bank's Beige Book.

FIGURE 1.5   Price Level Analysis: Daily Bar Chart.
Most of the 15-minute bar chart is contracted into the single right-most bar
of the daily chart.
Source: FXtrek IntelliChart™. Copyright 2001–2007 FXtrek.com, Inc.

TABLE 1.1 The Technical Market Paradigm

The theory of technical analysis states that all information relevant to the market is contained in the price data. Even volume and open interest statistics (not available to FOREX traders unless artificially synthesized from price data) are secondary to price data.

SYMBOL	USD	EUR	GBP	CAD	AUD	JPY	ZAR	CHF
USD		0.75002	0.50769	1.16061	1.2349	118.053	7.2124	1.2156
EUR	1.3329		0.67673	1.5467	1.6449	157.36	9.6155	1.6204
GBP	1.9692	1.4769		2.2854	2.4309	232.45	14.196	2.3936
CAD	0.86125	0.6465	0.43732		1.063	101.686	6.2148	1.0468
AUD	0.8098	0.6073	0.4111	0.9396		95.59	5.8427	0.9842
JPY	0.0085	0.0064	0.0043	0.00983	0.01045		0.0611	1.0287
ZAR	0.13832	0.10379	0.0703	0.16069	0.17088	16.349001		0.16834
CHF	0.8226	0.6171	0.4175	0.95449	1.015	97.07	5.9339	

Source: www.TradingCharts.com.

- Bridge/Commodity Research Bureau (CRB) indexes.
- BTM-UBSW Chain-Store Sales Index.
- Building permits.
- Business inventories.
- Capacity utilization.
- Capital flows, per Treasury International Capital System (TIC).
- Confederation of British Industry (CBI) report.
- Challenger, Gray, and Christmas layoff announcements.
- Chicago Purchasing Managers Index (PMI).
- Chicago Purchasing Managers Survey.
- Chartered Institute of Purchasing and Supply (CIPS) report.
- Composite Index of Leading Economic Indicators.
- Consumer confidence.
- Consumer installment credit.
- Consumer price index (CPI).
- Consumer sentiment.
- Consumer spending.
- Corporate profits.

- Current account (balance of payments).
- Durable goods orders.
- Employment cost index.
- Employment report.
- Employment situation.
- Existing home sales.
- Export prices.
- Factory orders.
- Federal budget.
- Federal government finances.
- Federal Reserve Policy disclosures.
- Financial account balance.
- Federal Open Market Committee (FOMC) minutes and transcripts.
- Foreign trade.
- GDP.
- GDP advance.
- GDP deflator.
- GDP final.
- GDP provisional (revised).
- GNP indicators.
- Goldman Sachs Commodity Index.
- Goldman Sachs Retail Index for Same-Store Sales.
- Help-wanted index.
- House prices.
- Housing starts.
- Humphrey-Hawkins testimony.
- German IFO index.
- Import prices.
- Industrial production.
- Industrial Production and Capacity Utilization report from Federal Reserve Board.
- Initial claims.
- International trade.
- Institute for Supply Management (ISM) Manufacturing Index.

- ISM Nonmanufacturing Survey.
- ISM Services Index.
- Jobless claims.
- Kansas City Federal Reserve Bank manufacturing survey.
- Lynch, Jones & Ryan (LJR) Redbook report.
- Manufacturers' shipments, inventories, and orders.
- Manufacturing and trade inventories.
- Michigan Consumer Sentiment Index (MCSI).
- Monetary base.
- Money supply figures (M1, M2, M3) released monthly by Federal Reserve Economic Data (FRED).
- Mortgage Bankers Association weekly survey.
- National Association of Purchasing Managers (NAPM) index.
- National Association of Home Builders (NAHB) survey.
- New home sales.
- Nonfarm payrolls.
- New York's Empire State Index.
- Orders, sectoral production, and inventories.
- Payroll employment.
- Personal consumption expenditures.
- Personal income.
- Philadelphia Fed index.
- Philadelphia Federal Reserve Bank Business Outlook Survey.
- Prices, wages, and productivity.
- Producer price index (PPI).
- Productivity.
- Purchasing Managers Index (PMI).
- Real earnings (real average weekly earnings).
- Real GDP.
- Redbook Index.
- Residential construction spending.
- Retail sales.
- Richmond Federal Reserve Bank Survey.
- Trade balance.
- Tankan report.

- Unemployment insurance claims.
- Unemployment rate.
- Unit auto and Ttuck sales.
- Unit labor cost.
- U.S. Treasury Borrowing Schedule.
- Wholesale inventories.

List courtesy of www.FOREXrealm.com.

Econometric Analysis

Econometric analysis attempts to convert fundamental data into pricing forecasts, most typically long-term forecasts. Because of the high leverage in FOREX, long-term forecasts may not be of value to many traders.

Econometric analysis typically yields complex mathematical/statistical models. Because of the complexity they are computer-based simulations.

The EXPO econometric software (www.lmt-expo.com) attempts shorter-term price forecasts, incorporating the following factors:

- *Data Transformations:* Box-Cox Transformations, Differencing, Logit, Seasonal Adjustment, and Periodicity Conversion.
- Statistical Analysis: Autocorrelation and Partial Autocorrelation Analysis, Q-statistics, Restricted Histogram, Correlation, and Variance/Covariance Matrix.
- Econometric Tests: Additional variables, superfluous variables, Dickey-Fuller Unit Root, Engle-Granger Cointegration, Granger Causality, Multicollinearity, Normality, LM Serial Correlation, GARCH and White Heteroskedasticity, Chow, and Ramsey.
- Model Estimation and Forecasting: OLS, GARCH, ARIMA, Ridge, rolling/moving regression, instrumental variables, and auto-regressive errors.
- Random Number Generation: Using Binomial, Chi-square, Exponential, F, Student-t, Normal, Lognormal, and Poisson Distributions.
- Frequency Analysis: Convolution, Discrete Fourier Transform, Fast Fourier Transform, Inverse Fourier Transforms, impulse

(Continued)

Econometric Analysis (*continued*)

filters, power spectral density, trigonometric functions generator, digital filter functions.

- Polynomial Analysis: Cubic spline interpolation, polynomial estimation, and statistics.

- Statistics: Summary statistics, rolling correlation and statistics; Student-t, F, ANOVA, and Chi-square tests.

- Mathematical Functions: An extensive set of advanced functions for matrix math and calculus are provided in EXPO's "Analyze" menu.

Courtesy of www.lmt-expo.com.

Why Technical Analysis?

Pay your money; take your pick. Technical analysis, despite its faults, has attracted more traders than fundamental analysis has, for the following reasons:

- Technical analysis input (primarily prices in FOREX) is objective, transparent, and available to everyone.

- Technical analysis offers a nearly infinite number of possibilities for manipulation and application. Despite the millions of hours of effort expended on technical analysis, the field is wide open. Who knows what you might discover?

- Technical analysis allows traders to see the markets at many different price levels—of their choosing—at the same time.

- Technical analysis lets traders easily time their entries and exits as well as monitor their trades while they are open and active.

If you are right using technical analysis, you will probably make money on a trade. If you are right using fundamental analysis, the leverage inherent in the market may well cause you to get stopped out or exit the trade before you can collect on your judgment.

Despite the fundamentalists' concept that prices used in technical analysis are "instant history," the technical market paradigm infers that actions in the market of buying and selling obviously have reactions in the markets of selling and buying. Past prices contain information about future prices. Whether this information can be usefully deciphered is an issue for the theorists.

Charting

Price charts of market behavior have been around for centuries, probably almost as long as markets have existed in both the East and West. The most important types of charts used today are bar charts, candlestick charts, point and figure charts, and swing charts.

All charts share the primary characteristic of visually depicting price behavior over some period of time. They differ as to their secondary characteristics and type and degree of visual impact.

Bar Charts

Bar charts are the most popular and enduring for all trading, whether stocks, options, futures, or FOREX. They are time-specific, meaning that they are scaled according to time increments. For FOREX this can be ticks: 5-second, 10-second, 30-second, 1-minute, 5-minute, 10-minute, 30-minute, 1-hour, 12-hour, daily, or weekly. See Figure 1.6.

Time-Specific versus Price-Specific
Charts constructed as a function of time units are said to be *time-specific*. For example, a bar chart using five-minute, daily, or weekly information is time specific. Point and figure charts are *price-specific*; they require only price unit information to construct them. Goodman Swing Charts are both time- and price-specific; information for both time and price is required.

Candlestick Charts

Candlestick charts, a charting idea from the East, are especially popular in FOREX. Candlestick chart patterns emphasize the technical analysis paradigm—that past prices carry information about future prices. Candlesticks are also time-specific.

I used candlestick charts in the 1980s to trade cocoon futures on the Japanese commodity exchange. When in Rome, do as the Romans do! See Figure 1.7.

Point and Figure Charts

Point and figure (P&F) charts have fallen from favor over the past 20 years. Perhaps this is a good reason to give them some extra consideration now. Point and figure charts are price-specific. Instead of scaling as a function of time,

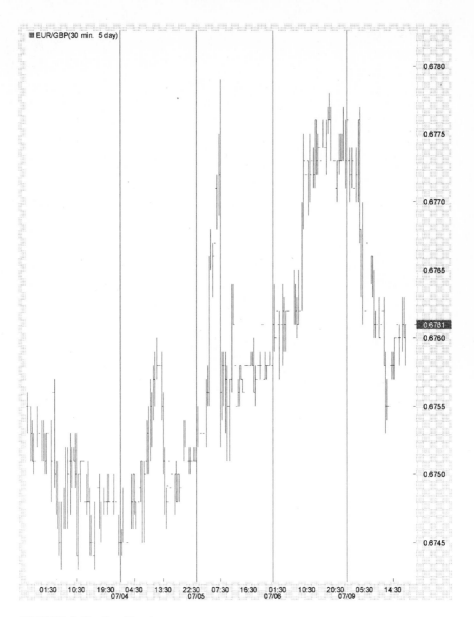

FIGURE 1.6 Bar Chart.
Source: FXtrek IntelliChart™. Copyright 2001–2007 FXtrek.com, Inc.

P&F charts are scaled as a function of price. In the end, it is a half-dozen of one and six of the other. Prices occur over time, and time is relevant only as it depicts changing prices.

It is said P&F charts were the "secret" of many of the robber barons of the nineteenth century who often raided railroad stocks using a tool no one else

FIGURE 1.7 Candlestick Chart.
Source: FXtrek IntelliChart™. Copyright 2001–2007 FXtrek.com, Inc.

used. I don't know how true that is, but it rings true to me. Trading tools invariably are most effective when they are not widely used. After a technique becomes popular, it loses much of its effectiveness. The theory is this: The market, never interested in cooperating with traders, essentially immunizes itself against overly popular techniques to prevent the masses from making money.

To understand the market's ability to discount and immunize itself, we need only to consider the commodity spread relationships in grain futures. Useful and effective in the 1950s and 1960s, they have shifted so dramatically as to be worthless today. See Figure 1.8.

Swing Charts

Swing charts can be either time-specific or price-specific, although most of them are price-specific in the manner of P&F charts. I like swing charts very much for my close-up view of markets when I am looking to enter or exit. They are also, obviously, useful for detecting swings in the market. When I discuss the FxCodex method of trading, you will see how important the information derived from swing charts can be to trading currencies. See Figure 1.9.

There is no best chart technique. Many traders use more than one for studying the markets. I use bar charts and swing charts and occasionally refer to point and figure charts. If you haven't selected a primary chart tool, look at the same market over the identical period of time with each type. Which one speaks to you? If you have already selected a charting technique, feel free to use it to develop your personal codex.

I strongly encourage a charting method as your primary tool both for watching the markets and for deriving buy and sell signals.

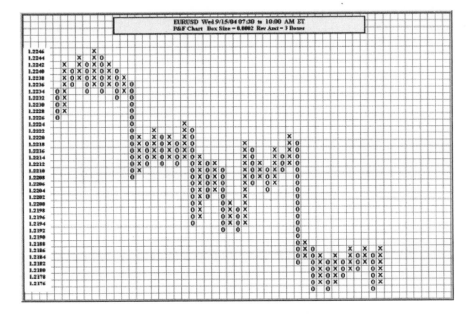

FIGURE 1.8 Point and Figure Chart.

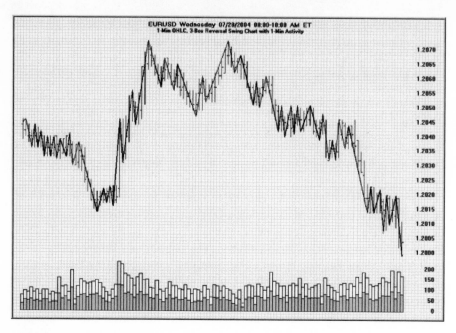

FIGURE 1.9   Swing Charts.

Indicators

Indicators are popular with traders. The classification and sheer variety of indicators is vast, and a full discussion of them is beyond the scope of this work. Because most of us aren't math and statistics experts, anything that uses dazzling displays of mathematical pyrotechnics often seems somehow magical and infallible to us.

Many traders use an indicator battery (IB), which is a selection of perhaps a dozen or more indicators covering all the technical bases. If you use an IB, you need to have ad hoc rules (or a meta-indicator or indicators) to determine what all of its components mean and how to apply them in actually executing a trade.

Charts offer traders a transparent one-to-one correspondence with market prices; indicators do not, and that is the primary problem with them. Indicators are second-level techniques. They use the primary market data such as prices but manipulate it to attain a new level, hopefully, of understanding.

Information theory tells us that such translations or manipulations are fraught with some risk and danger. Without being 100 percent certain how the indicator relates to the underlying data, we can be easily misled. Markets move in prices, and using indicators requires that we constantly shift levels to make trading decisions. Each shift can cause an error, and because the markets move very swiftly, errors compound quickly.

Indicators also tend to be curve-fit. That is, you must somehow select time frames and other parameters to calculate the indicator value. As the markets change, these parameters may need to be constantly altered and updated. Trending markets evolve—sometimes rather quickly—into trading markets, and vice versa. Some indicators do this internally, after a fashion. For others—you guessed it—you need another indicator to make those decisions.

Indicators are opaque to varying degrees. The more complex the indicator the more difficult it is to determine what it is really measuring. In the meantime, the markets are marching onward and upward or downward. Another consequence of this opaqueness is that it is difficult to develop rational money-management tools using most indicators because the primary-level connection to prices has been severed in the calculation process. Stops, for example, are a function of prices, and your indicator needs to convert its findings back to price levels to determine a stop. Of course, you can always build another indicator to do that for you. If you've guessed that I'm not a big fan of indicators, you are correct.

Figures 1.10 through 1.12 provide examples of the three most common types of indicators—moving averages, oscillators, and relative strength.

Cycle Analysis

If the technical market paradigm is correct, then prices have a memory of some sort. *Cycle analysis* accepts this as an axiom and takes the idea a small step further: Prices behave in cycles. There is certainly logic to this, I think. But whether the markets are cyclical in nature or simply exhibit cyclical behavior from time to time is the big question.

Components of a Cycle

All cycles are defined by four parameters:

1. Amplitude—the distance between the maximum or minimum value and the mean value of the cycle; half the vertical range.
2. Wavelength—the period of the cycle as measured from one peak to the next peak or from one trough to the next trough.
3. Phase—the horizontal shift left or right for a cycle.
4. Decay/expansion—cycles may decay or expand for the above values over time, either linearly or nonlinearly.

Markets, if they have cyclical aspects, must certainly have multiple cycles. Small cycles represent the shortest-term traders; intermediate cycles

FIGURE 1.10 Popular Indicators: Exponential Moving Average.
Source: FXtrek IntelliChart™. Copyright 2001–2007 FXtrek.com, Inc.

represent the next level of traders; and large cycles represent long-term traders—the latter even exist in FOREX. There are perhaps dozens of levels in between.

Theoretically, if you sum all the cycles inherent in a market—again, assuming they are even there—you will get a summed cycle that has the same peaks and valleys as the underlying market. See Figure 1.13.

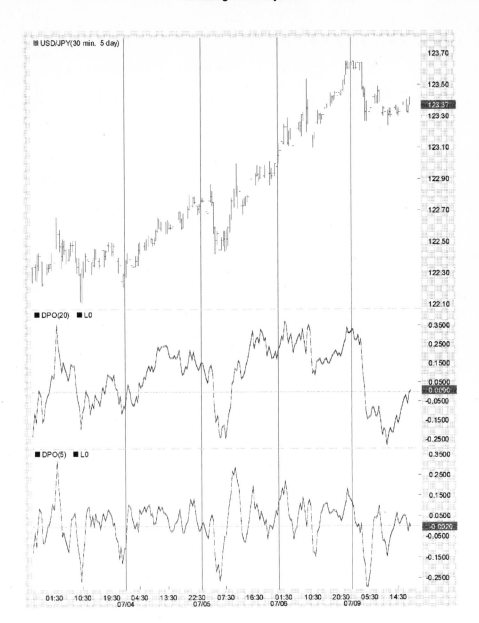

FIGURE 1.11 Popular Indicators: Oscillator (Bollinger Band).
Source: FXtrek IntelliChart™. Copyright 2001–2007 FXtrek.com, Inc.

Behavior Analysis

Behavior analysis takes another tack in accessing the technical market paradigm. Its central concept is focused on the behavior and propensities of traders. According to the behaviorists, their activities of buying and selling can be profitably measured and monitored. See Figure 1.14.

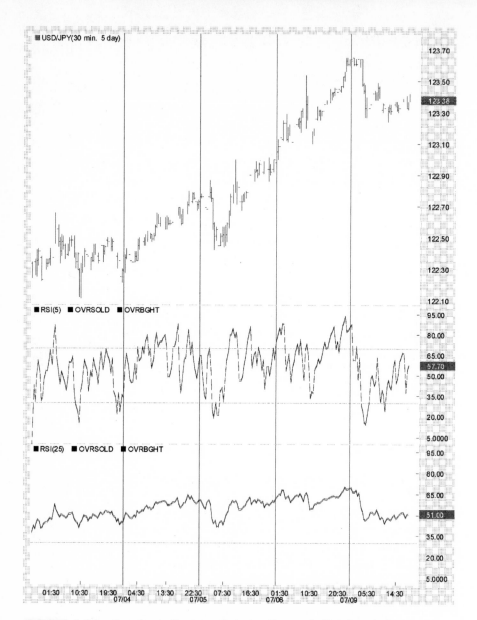

FIGURE 1.12 Popular Indicators: Relative Strength (Stochastics)
Source: FXtrek IntelliChart™. Copyright 2001–2007 FXtrek.com, Inc.

Much of the data for behavior studies derives from trading volume and open interest. *Trading volume* is the gross number of trades made over some period of time. *Open interest* is the total number of buyers and sellers in the market as a function of whether they are *new* buyers and sellers over some period or *old* buyers and sellers already in the market.

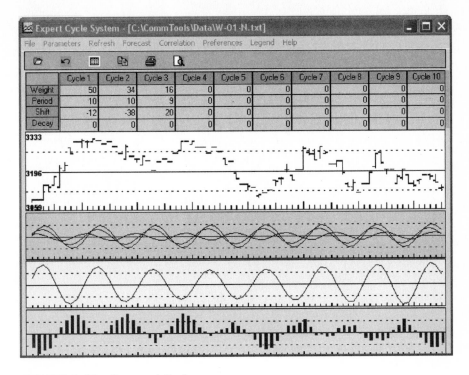

FIGURE 1.13 Summed Cycles.
The three cycles in the middle of the chart are summed to create the cycle just below it.
Source: Expert Cycle System (www.FxPraxis.com).

Volume and Open Interest

Because there is no central clearinghouse for currency trading, there are no aggregate volume or open interest statistics. In theory, this information could be synthesized from price data.

Volume is the total number of transactions (buy/sell) over a period of time. *Open interest* is the total number of trades open and active at a given time in a specific quantity unit.

Volume and open interest in futures are classically interpreted as shown in the following table:

Price	Volume	Open Interest	Interpretation
Rising	Rising	Rising	Market is strong.
Rising	Falling	Falling	Market is weakening.
Falling	Rising	Rising	Market is weak.
Falling	Falling	Falling	Market is strengthening.

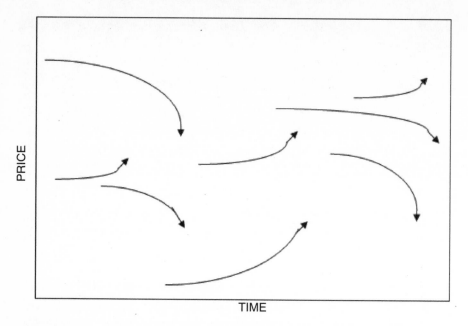

FIGURE 1.14   The Ultimate Trading Paradigm.
Every trader in the market has a propensity to exit the market at some combination of price and time. Every trader contemplating entering the market has a propensity for some price and time. The sum total of these propensities or decisions constitutes the flow of prices over time.

Behavior analysis is less useful in FOREX than in futures or options. There is no centralized exchange or clearinghouse and thus no reporting of total volume or tracking of open interest.

Because I have a high opinion of behavior analysis, I have spent a considerable amount of effort devising *synthetic volume* and *synthetic open interest* to provide analogous data for currency behavior analysis studies. For more information on this research, you may want to visit my web site, www.FxPraxis.com.

Market Filters

Market filters, in general, are statistical tools indicating possible high-risk trading areas or times. Because of the leverage and pace in FOREX trading, filters can be extremely useful. If a filter prevents you from making a single bad trade, it has paid the cost of having it in your toolbox.

Here is a simple example of a useful filter: The Federal Reserve makes routine (and sometimes not so routine) pronouncements at 8:30 A.M. Eastern

Standard Time. The markets—those involving the USD—often react very violently just after such announcements (as you will see in Figure 1.16). Pull up some charts of this time of day and see for yourself. Observe how often the market feints in one direction right after the announcement and then proceeds in the opposite direction soon thereafter. Don't enter a trade just before a Fed announcement. Do watch the action after an announcement. See Figures 1.15 and 1.16.

After you decide which pairs and crosses you will trade, it is important to develop and keep a calendar of relevant events and announcements for the country in question. Serious traders will also follow general events in that country for clues to news that may impact its currency.

Your daily trade plan should include a calendar showing any such scheduled announcements. Not stepping in doo-doo is more important than finding the pot of gold at the end of the rainbow. The pot of gold is always there, but if you lose too much money you will no longer be in the race to find it.

Whereas fundamentals may be difficult to use, news is not. News provides important feedback about the market. A market's reaction to news may yield valuable clues as to the underlying strength or weakness of a currency. I say more about using news in Part 3.

The Toolbox Approach

A typical toolbox takes tools from several categories:

- Charts, including:
  - Bar Charts
  - Swing Charts
  - Point & Figure Charts
  - Candlestick Charts
  - Indicators—the list is long, but most can be reduced to these categories:
- Moving averages
  - Oscillators
  - Bands
  - Stochastics
- Cycles
  - Market filters

The traditional trader will generally pull techniques from all these categories. That is both good and bad. It is good because more information for making intelligent trading decisions is at your fingertips. It is bad because the more techniques you use, the more opaque your trading strategy becomes. The more opaque your strategy—the further away you get from the actual

Forex Calendar: Economic Indicator and Central Bank Dates

FX Monthly Calendar updated weekly - - FX Schedule

All times GMT-

Mon, Jul 9, 2007
23:50 JA- May core machinery orders
23:50 JA- Jun M2+CDs
06:00 DE- May Trade
08:30 UK- Jun PPI
08:30 UK- Jun Trade
10:00 DE- May Ind Prod
19:00 US- May Consumer Credit

Tue, Jul 10, 2007
09:30 UK- Jun Trade
13:00 CA- BOC Policy Announcement
14:00 US- May Wholesale Trade (see +0.4% vs. +0.3%)

Wed, Jul 11, 2007
JA- BOJ meeting -- day one
23:50 JA- May C/A
23:50 JA- Jun Corp Goods Prices
09:30 UK- Jun Trade
14:30 US- Weekly Enegy

Thu, Jul 12, 2007
JA- BOJ meeting -- day two
00:30 AU- June Employment
05:30 JA- May final IP
09:00 EZ- May IP
10:00 EZ- 1Q07 GDP (2d release)
12:30 US- Weekly Claims
12:30 US- May Trade (see -$60bn vs. -$58.5bn)
12:30 CA- May Trade
18:00 US- Jun Budget

Fri, Jul 13, 2007
12:30 US- Jun Retail Sales (see +0.4% vs. +1.4%; ex-autos +0.4% vs. +1.3%)
14:00 US- May Business Inventories (see +0.3% vs. +0.4%)
14:00 US- Jul prelim UM sentiment (see 85.5 vs. 85.3)

FIGURE 1.15   Fed Announcements.
For those trading the USD versus any other currency, the announcements by the Federal Reserve are critical. These announcements very often elicit high volatility and extreme price movements, at least for a few minutes of trading. Most broker/dealer trading platforms have an economic calendar with all important news and announcements listed. One excellent resource is www.ForexEconomicCalendar.com.
Source: www.global-view.com.

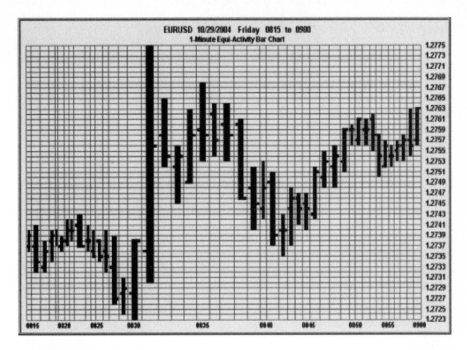

FIGURE 1.16 Shockwaves

prices going by on your trading platform screen—the more difficult it is to know what you are actually seeing and measuring. Consequently, it becomes more difficult to convert that plethora of information to an actual trade. The markets move quickly and it is very easy to get lost in your own toolbox. By the time you find your hammer, some other trader has driven the nail home.

Select tools that complement and supplement each other. If you use indicators, don't use four different oscillators and no moving average; if you do, you've left out a good trending market tool. If you use charts, don't use both point and figure and swing charts—they overlap too much.

Toolbox Configuration

A no-nonsense, classical toolbox configuration might look like this:
Charts
  Bar charts
Indicators
  Moving averages
  Oscillators
Market Filters
  Time-of-day studies
  Announcements and news

Summary

This chapter is intended to give you a very brief overview of traditional trading techniques as a trading *element*—their pluses and minuses individually and collectively. The field of technical analysis is vast and enormously interesting. This is certainly one reason that most traders spend most of their time and effort here. The resources of technical analysis are staggering, and the possibilities—for better or for worse—are endless.

More specific information is presented in Parts 2 and 3 for those tools selected for the FxCodex method. The codex approach folds trading techniques into an analytical *process* and they become less important individually than they are to the traditional trader.

Don't let the sheer quantity of information confuse or mislead you. Trading tools are only one-third of the successful trader's set of elements. Money management and the soft elements are just as important, perhaps more so. The alluring siren song of trading techniques has been the ruin of many, many traders.

Let the trader beware!

Chapter

2

The Soft Elements of Style

If it looks like a fish, be sure it can swim.

—Charles B. Goodman

By *soft elements* I mean those elements less subject to objective criteria and more dependent on a trader's own personal and subjective likes and dislikes. Soft elements include the trader profile, market selection, tactics, and psychology and attitude. Taken together, the soft elements define a trader's *style*.

These elements are given in-depth consideration when I develop the codex process approach to trading in Part Three of *Getting Started in FOREX Trading Strategies (GSIFTS)*. But a brief introduction here is useful. Even traditional traders must have answers to the soft elements, although they are often given much less consideration than trading techniques. Decide and define your style before trading. By positioning yourself appropriately in the market, many trading decisions will be easier to make. Diagnosing problem areas is also a simpler task if you "know thyself."

Even though these elements are relatively nonobjective, they cannot be irrational, hodgepodge, or contradictory. For the best chance of trading success, they should complement each other as well as your trading techniques and money management decisions.

You may well need to go back and fill in some soft element answers after digesting the decisions required in Chapter 3, "Money Management."

Style

Style is the sum of nonquantifiable decisions you make regarding your trading plan. They include, but are not limited to, the markets you trade (your focus: short term, intermediate term, long term); the kinds of markets you prefer (trading markets, trending markets); and your attitude and outlook on trading.

Style is the cumulative sum of the soft elements defining you as a trader. How much do you trade? Do you like fast markets or slow markets? Trading markets or trending markets? Do you seek big moves or small moves? Are you happy with a 10 pip winner, or do you need 100 pips? In which markets have you been most successful? These are personal decisions with no right or wrong answers, but again, they must complement each other and be realistic.

With dozens of pairs and crosses and around-the-clock trading, there is plenty of action in FOREX, so there's never a reason for trading markets less than suitable to the trader's style.

Market Environments

A *market environment* (ME) is a rating, either quantified or judgmental, about a market's directional movement and volatility. It is a key element of the codex approach; it impacts trading across a wide range of decisions regarding trading techniques, money management, and style.

Studying markets and trades in the framework of market environments is a critical codex functionality. Two factors defining market analysis will tell you the current personality of any market. All markets can be deconstructed into *directional movement* and *volatility*.

Directional Movement

Which way is the market going, up or down? And how quickly over time is it rising or falling? There are different ways to measure directional movement (DM) but it is basically the slope of the line or the price differential from the beginning point of a trend to the end point of that trend. I prefer the price differential for eyeballing, Charlie-style.

In the example shown in Figure 2.1, I would take raw DM = 5 units, based on the close of the first bar and the close of the final bar.

For eyeballing I use a range of 1 to 4 and a label of up or down. I visualize a price movement of 100 percent (a vertical line) as 4 and a price movement of 0 percent (a horizontal line) as 1, then picture the data as potentially comprising four 25 percent quartiles.

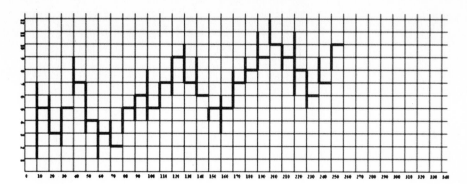

FIGURE 2.1 Directional Movement.

Any number of ideas and notations will work just fine; use what is comfortable for you. In my system, "1D" means a market is falling very slowly, while "4U" means it is rising very quickly. Other notations are fine, as long as usage is consistent. The idea is to build a catalogue of examples for study, analysis, and hypothesis testing. For example, simply using a range of 1 to 8 would work well, also.

If you believe you can be objective and consistent, you might not even want to use numbers and instead go with simply high, medium, and low.

In Figure 2.1 with its raw DM = 5, I rate the overall DM as 2, closer to 1 and to 0 percent change in price than to 4 and 100 percent change in price.

Volatility

Volatility (V) is defined as the "price action over a trend (directional movement) over and above the absolute value of the trend."

While DM is the net price change, volatility is the total of all price changes over a trend, given some minimum fluctuation, and divided by DM. For example, if DM = 10 and V = 30, then raw volatility = 3.

Volatility is a little more difficult to scale and notate. Through experience I've found it measures typically 200 percent to 1,000 percent of DM, although it can go much higher. The longer your chart sample and the smaller the price fluctuations it records, the larger percentage for volatility. With that you can use the same notation as for DM, with 1 representing low volatility and 4 representing high volatility.

In the example in Figure 2.2, raw DM = 5 units and raw V = 40. Volatility is 8 times the DM, or 800 percent. Given a potential range, as I said, of 200 to 1,000 percent, I would rate V as 3.

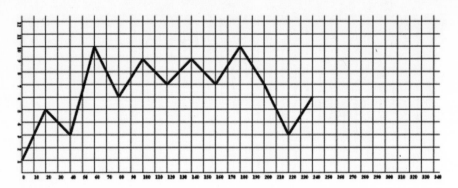

FIGURE 2.2 Volatility.

How you measure and notate any of the elements is not as important as ensuring that the measurements are consistent. There are statistical methods for measuring V and all of the elements but they are beyond the scope of this article. It is not difficult to accurately eyeball volatility once you get some practice on a few dozen charts.

Market Selection

Market selection is a vital codex element and is covered in more detail in Parts 2 and 3 of *GSIFTS*. The most popular markets are those involving the U.S. dollar (USD); these are called *pairs*. The euro (EUR) against the U.S. dollar (EUR/USD) dwarfs all others in trading volume.

A *pair* is a set of traded currencies with the USD as one of the components. A *cross* is a set of currencies without the USD as a component. See Table 2.1.

What pairs or crosses do you trade? Some markets are more volatile than others; each market has its own, slowly evolving personality occasionally

TABLE 2.1 Most Frequently Traded Currency Pairs

The new trader is advised to focus on USD majors and move on to cross rates only after mastering the majors.

USD Majors	Cross Rates
EUR/USD	EUR/CHF
GBP/USD	EUR/JPY
USD/CHF	EUR/GBP
USD/JPY	GBP/JPY
AUD/USD	CHF/JPY

impacted by news events. As you'll see in the sections that follow, day traders and the position traders will be attracted to low-volatility trending markets that can be managed over longer periods of time. Guerillas and scalpers will seek out high-volatility trading markets offering fast but small profits.

Market Characteristics

Each market, irrespective of its placement as a specific pair or cross, is a function of the two basic market environment factors—directional movement and volatility. A third factor can be added. I call it *thickness* (T). Thickness refers to the amount of overlap between the high and low price of one trading unit and the next trading unit. The more overlap, the thicker the market is said to be. I very much like and seek thick markets and have had great success trading them both in futures and in FOREX.

Thickness can be measured as the average overlap from one price bar to the next on a chart, averaged over a given period of time. Thick markets are recommended to beginning traders.

I simply use high, medium, and low as my labels for eyeballing thickness. In Figure 2.3, the market on the left demonstrates high thickness, the one in the middle is medium thickness, and on the right, low thickness or *thin*.

You can also do something similar for T as for DM and V. Take raw T to be 0 when there is no overlap and 100 when there is 100 percent overlap, and break the data into four 25 percent quartiles. An outside day, where both highs are higher and lows are lower, would still be rated simply as 100 percent raw T.

Where price bars have little overlap, they are said to run thin. Fast-trending markets tend to be thin.

Remember you are using the average thickness over the trend or chart you are analyzing. Thickness, fortunately, tends to change slowly, so this is not a major issue.

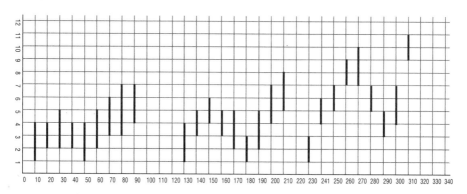

FIGURE 2.3 Thickness.

The Trader Profile

Perhaps the most important soft question is also the easiest to answer: At what level of trading do you feel most at home? Although levels are a continuum and not easily separated, four basic levels can be considered: guerilla, scalper, day trader, and position trader. Recognizing your trading level is the first step in defining a *trader profile*.

A trader's profile is the decision to trade short-term, intermediate-term, or long-term markets. Very short-term traders are *guerillas*, short-term traders are *scalpers*, intermediate term traders are *day traders*, and long-term traders are *position traders*.

The orientation in FOREX is even shorter than it is in futures. Very few traders are position traders in FOREX; the risk of staying over from one session to the next is very high. Guerillas are also called high-frequency traders—and, of course, the brokers love them!

My recommendation: Focus on being either a scalper or day trader. See Figure 2.4.

Guerillas

The *guerilla* traders are the shortest-term traders. They look for the quickest in-and-out possible. A profit of 5 to 20 pips is their trading goal. Caution: Unless

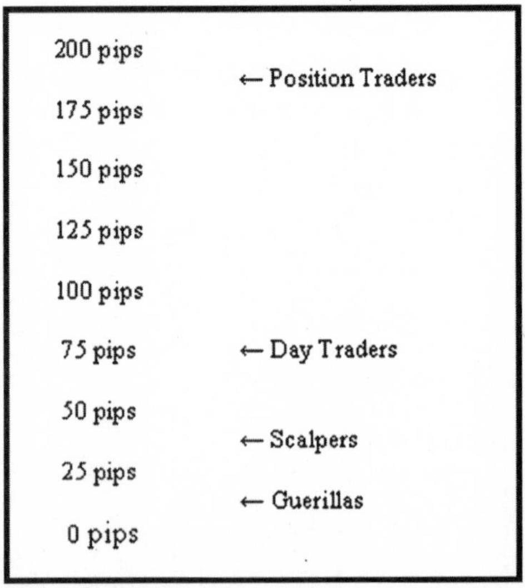

```
200 pips
              ← Position Traders
175 pips

150 pips

125 pips

100 pips

75 pips         ← Day Traders

50 pips
              ← Scalpers
25 pips
              ← Guerillas
0 pips
```

FIGURE 2.4 Basic Trader Profiles.
There is risk inherent in simply being in the market. The longer you stay, the greater the risk. Therefore, longer-term traders must seek greater rewards to compensate for the risk. A guerilla trader should rarely be in a trade for more than 15 to 30 minutes.

you trade large numbers and receive extremely small bid-ask spreads from your broker/dealer, the guerilla approach is *not* recommended.

Scalpers

The *scalpers* are close cousins of the guerillas. They seek profits in the 10 to 40 pip range. If you have a small account and want to be a scalper, stay with the most liquid pairs where pip spreads are small. A 3-pip spread does not sound like much but, as you will see in Chapter 3, it can eat you alive quickly. The more you trade, the greater a factor trading costs will become to you.

Day Traders

The *day traders* want trades with a potential of 20 to100 pips. They obviously trade less than either the guerilla or the scalper. If you want to be a day trader, you need to use stops, know that they are in effect, or stay online while your trade is live. I prefer the day trader profile but, again, it is a personal decision with no right or wrong answer.

Day traders will often stay with an active trade across multiple trading sessions, but rarely more than 24 hours. See Figure 2.5.

Position Traders

The *position traders* are rare creatures in the FOREX arena. They are willing to keep a trade open across two or more trading days. Like the day traders, position traders need to use stops consistently or stay awake as long as a trade is

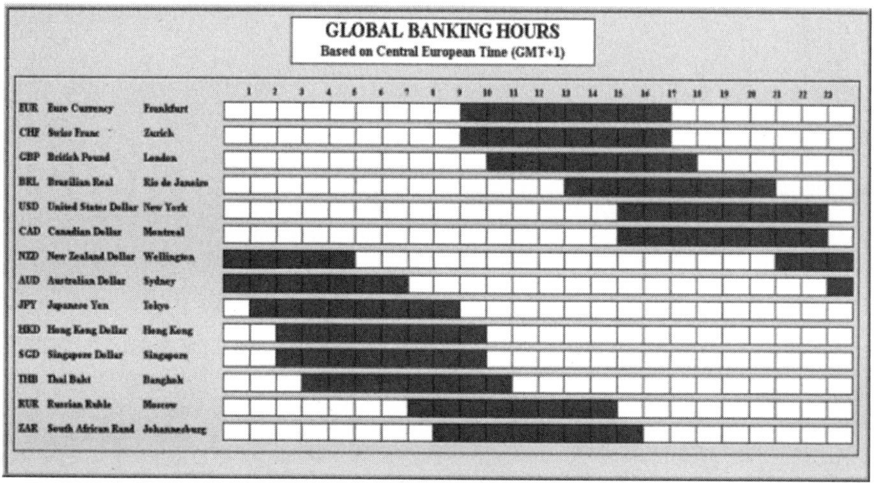

FIGURE 2.5 Trading Sessions.
FOREX sessions are also divided into the U.S. session, the European session, and the Asian session.

live. These traders trade the least and grab the biggest profits. But the downside is risk: The longer you are in a trade, the riskier it becomes because of trade-shattering news events or announcements that can quickly destroy a carefully nurtured position.

Psychology and Attitude

Some people have a naturally winning attitude. Others are self-destructive. Nothing brings out that trait faster than leveraged markets such as FOREX. If you don't have a naturally winning attitude you can develop one, but it is not easy. If you are self-destructive, your chances of success in the markets are not good.

Psychology in trading is primarily about keeping your emotions in check. The primary emotions of any market trader are fear and greed. The more leveraged and volatile a market, the quicker these emotions can harm your efforts. If you trade stocks with zero leverage, these emotions may not affect your trading performance very often or even critically. In FOREX they will come at you every single trading session.

Your psychology and attitude should be reflected in many of your codex decisions. The exceptionally nervous trader is not a candidate to be a good position trader; it would be better for the nervous trader to scalp the markets and alleviate the worry coming from holding a position a long time.

Universally, successful traders are able to keep their emotions out of their trading decisions—and it is *not* easy to do. Keep but move.

In Part Two, I detail more specific aspects of psychology and attitude and how they relate to building a personal trading codex.

Fear and Greed

It is said that fear and greed move the markets. When a market is trending up, the buyers are greedy and the sellers are fearful. When the market is trending down, the sellers are greedy and the buyers are fearful. A chart of prices is also a chart of these emotions in action.

I have found the old 1960s technique of biofeedback to be very useful. Keep a chart of your emotions at different points of each trading session and observe how they tend to move with the market—or, more specifically, with your position in the market. Just knowing that this is happening is the best

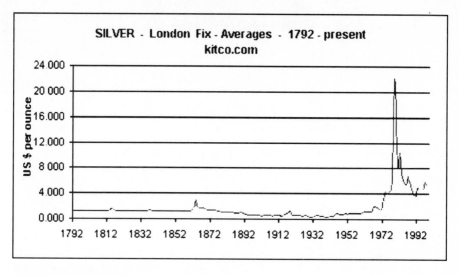

FIGURE 2.6 Charting Fear and Greed.
Greed: In 1973 the Hunt brothers (Nelson Bunker and William Herbert) began taking delivery on silver futures contracts. *Fear:* In early 1980, silver peaked at $54 per ounce, then plummeted on March 17 from $21.62 to $10.80 in a single day.

defense against intruding emotions. If you can't check your emotions, it is perfectly fine to walk away for a while. The markets and the opportunities will always be there when you return, whether you come back after a few minutes or a few months. See Figure 2.6.

Tactics

This book is about strategy, but tactics are also vital to trading success. If strategy is the plan, *tactics* are the execution. Strategy will lead to the pot of gold; tactics will deliver it to your house.

Market filters and a close monitoring of the effects of news on the markets, as discussed in Chapter 1, can be considered tactics. You may have a great trade all laid out, but if the Fed makes an unexpected announcement, it may all be for naught.

The tactics of a trade often determine whether you should get right back in a trade if you are stopped out, or whether you should wait for the factors that made the trade promising to you to realign themselves.

Record keeping is also a tactic. Both a daily and a weekly trading plan are important. The currency markets move so rapidly that you simply must have a complete set of contingency plans at your fingertips at all times.

> ### Contingency Planning
>
> Never begin a trading session without knowing what you will do in a number of different scenarios. The markets move quickly, leverage is high, and taking time to make a decision adds to trade risk. This holds true for trades in which you have an active position and trades you are contemplating entering. Ask yourself the following questions:
>
> - What if the market opens higher and moves lower?
> - What if the market opens lower and moves higher?
> - What if the market collapses?
> - What if the market soars?
> - What if volatility changes dramatically?
> - What if I am stopped out?
> - What if my profit objective is met?
> - Under what conditions would I alter my stop or profit objective?

Summary

Traditional traders generally do not give enough consideration to the soft elements and never develop a coherent trading style. Their style is generally a hodgepodge of experience and ad hoc ideas, if it exists in any form. The codex approach considers style an equal partner with trading techniques and money management. A coherent trading style that derives from specific pretrade choices gives the trader a framework for making the intelligent and quick decisions necessary in the FOREX arena.

Chapter 3

Money Management

Sit on your hands, Dad; sit on your hands!

—Charles B. Goodman

Money management is the art of breaking even! At least that is what my mentor, Charles B. Goodman, always told me. Even a blind squirrel gathers a few nuts. If you are in the game long enough, the nuts will find you. If you lose money and are shown the door, someone else will gather them. The first step to being around for nut time is breaking even.

Most traders lose; if they broke even they would still be in the game. If you're not in the game, you can't win.

Although profit maximization should be an important element in your money management plans, it is clear that risk avoidance is more critical. A real loss carries more weight than a potential profit.

Of the three trading elements, money management is perhaps the most important. Sadly, it is not given such status by most traders, nor does the literature accurately indicate its place in successful trading. If you have a mediocre trading technique, good money management can make it successful, or at least keep you from getting hurt. But if your money management is poor, the best techniques available won't save you from ruin in the long run.

I've already written about the concepts of transparency and opaqueness, and I say more about them in Parts 2 and 3. These concepts also apply to money management. The more transparent and connected to the actual markets your money management techniques are, the better. Opaqueness spells failure for money management. I once knew a trader who simply entered and exited the market on indicator signals, without reference to actual market prices or actions. He did not last long. The indicator approach to entry and exit caused him to accept small profits and stand for large losses.

To some degree, money management has to be subjective. The markets do strange things, and when you have an open position, reality sometimes demands action—rules or no rules. Nonetheless, an objective, rule-based money management codex is a required starting point. In most cases, even ad hoc subjective decisions can be made within the context of your codex.

Because most traditional traders focus on trading techniques, money management is too often an ad hoc effort. Money management is typically a set of rules for entry and exit, most often comprised merely of stops to get out of a bad trade before too much capital erosion has occurred. Profits are taken when it feels right or when the trader gets nervous. Intuition is fine, but it should be only supplemental to your defined trading codex.

Risk and Reward

Traders should consider three primary ratios within the context of what type of trader they are—or hope to become. The biggest single error is mismatching these ratios with the selected trading profile and/or the characteristics of the market being traded.

You can't be a scalper making 20 pips on a good trade and factor in losing 60 percent of your trades. The cost of trading is too high. It is nearly impossible to limit losses in FOREX to less than 10 pips, costs included. A position trader may be elated to make a 100 pip trade. But if this occurs in only 1 trade out of 20, that trader is finished anyway. See Table 3.1.

The bigger your average trade objective, the less you can afford on aggregate account drawdown; if you make two or three losing trades you will dig a hole from which it will be difficult or impossible to recover. The lower the ratio between your specific trade win-loss percent, the higher must be your aggregate win-loss percent. I have seen many traders fail simply because they denied the reality of these basic money management concepts.

		TABLE 3.1 Do the Math	
Average Trade Objective	Aggregate Account Drawdown	Win-to-Loss Percentage of Specific Trades	Aggregate Win-to-Loss Percentage
25 pips	50%	1:1	5:1
50 pips	33%	2:1	4:1
100 pips	25%	3:1	3:1

The three ratios that need to be considered are:

1. Aggregate account drawdown or risk.
2. Win-to-loss percentage for specific trades.
3. Aggregate percentage of wins to losses.

The parameters and ratios you set for money management *must* work together in harmony. They must also be in sync with your trading profile. For example, you can't expect to have a 10:1 winning ratio of trades with a maximum 5-pip loss per trade. Part Two details these ratios for the codex approach.

In the accompanying box are two more examples to give you a sense of how these ratios interact. The position trader can live with perhaps a 30 percent win-to-loss ratio if the trader is nailing 100-pip trades and limiting losses to 25 pips. The guerilla needs to achieve success on a very high number of trades because of the low ratio between winning trades and losing trades.

A Successful Position Trader

A basic concept for all traders is that the lower the ratio between your individual wins and losses (or profit objectives and stops, as realized), the higher the ratio of aggregate wins and losses must be.

A successful position trader:

- Has an average individual win/loss ratio of 5:1. This means for every $1 he loses in a trade, he makes $5.

- Has an average aggregate win/loss ratio of 1:3. This means for every one winning trade he has three losing trades.

Do the math: Out of 20 trades, 5 are winners and 15 are losers. On the losing trades he is out $1 x 15 trades = $15. On the winning trades he is profitable $5 x 5 trades = $25.

Consider a guerilla whose individual win/loss ratio is 1:1. He wins $1 for every $1 he loses. A 1:3 aggregate ratio puts him out of business very quickly.

Ceteris paribus (that is, all other things being equal), the position trader must be capitalized better than the scalper. Capital clout is required in order to stay with a position over multiple trading sessions. It takes time for 100- to 200-pip profits to accrue.

After you've ascertained your trading profile, grab a calculator and play "what if" with each of the three ratios. In Part Three you'll need to put these in stone, but for now just get a feel for how they work or don't work together.

Analyzing your trades vis-à-vis these ratios can tell you a lot about your trading performance—your strengths as well as your weaknesses. By keeping statistics on each trade and also a running total, the codex trader can make adjustments as necessary before disaster strikes. As a diagnostic tool, money management is the financial analysis of FOREX trading.

Entry

How do you enter a market? Does the signal come from your trading technique? Probably. It does for most traders, traditional or codex. That's the easy part. Every trader is fully focused when it is time to enter a market.

Trade or Pass

- Does the trade fall into my trader profile?
- Does it meet my money management criteria such as the ratio between my profit objective and my stop loss?
- Is the market environment (volatility, directional movement, thickness) suitable to me? How have I done in previous trades with the same ME profiles?
- How have I done in the past in this market (i.e., EUR/USD)?
- Have I been planning this trade or did it just attract me this trading session?
- Am I excited or calm?

When you enter a trade, even if it is a go from the perspective of trading technique and style, it should be a no-go if the money management ratios don't look right and in alignment with your trading profile. This is where sitting on your hands separates the pros from the amateurs. It is not easy to pass up a trade that looks good simply because the risk/reward is poor.

Exit

Exiting a trade is often a more complex matter. Determination of the timing may or may not come solely from a trading technique; many techniques do not have exits built in, and some degree of ad hoc measures is needed. There is nothing wrong with this, but unless your trading tools tell you when to exit, you need to have your ratios ready and waiting.

This is another reason to select your trades wisely. When a trade is active, your flexibility as to decision making falls dramatically.

The simplest form of exiting is a stop; correctly placing a stop requires thought and effort.

Stops

Stops are an unfortunate necessity of trading life. FOREX markets move so quickly that you must enter stops when you enter your trade. Most trading platforms today offer this capability, including scaling stops, and the technique is easy to learn and manage.

Basic Stop-Loss Techniques

The type of stop-loss orders varies from one broker-dealer to another. It is important to remember what standing orders you have in the market at all times. Most trade stations show you a record of all your open orders in the market.

Stop-losses may be entered in one of three ways:

1. As a function of price alone. This is the simplest for new traders. Use your trader profile ratios to set a stop-loss as a function of your profit objective.
2. According to the tenets of your technical trading method(s).
3. Above or below support and resistance points.

If you use the third method, remember that many traders use some form of support and resistance analysis. Despite the variety of support and resistance methods, most of them cluster in very similar price areas. Professional traders often use those areas to make contrarian trades—they are buying and selling when your stops are being hit. See Figure 3.1.

No one enjoys having stops sitting in the market, just waiting to be hit by a market whipsaw. It happens, and to everyone. If it happens too often, you will need to make adjustments somewhere in your ratios. Perhaps your stop is too close, in relationship to either your trade profile or the volatility of the market. If a market is moving 20 pips in five minutes, a 5-pip stop may be unrealistic.

You don't need a computer or a calculator to place stops effectively; common sense trumps everything. See Figure 3.2.

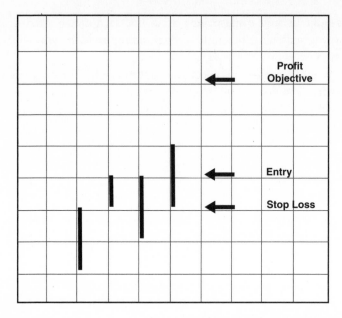

FIGURE 3.1 Basic Stop-Loss Techniques: Using Ratios to Calculate Stops.

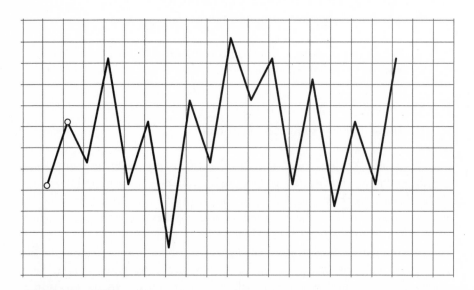

FIGURE 3.2 Whipsaw.

In market environments with *low* directional movement and *high* volatility, it is very difficult to set rational stops. These markets should be traded simply by their inherent rhythm—or avoided. Stops in this example would be impossible to set rationally.

Traders easily panic when stops get hit too frequently; that's when emotions can take control of your trading. That may be the time to walk away from trading for a while.

Traders tend to be more objective when entering a market than when exiting. Exiting means your money is on the line and your emotions are more likely to want a say in your decision.

The market is always attempting to get us to second-guess ourselves. If you catch yourself second-guessing too often, *stop trading*. The market has you where it wants you and is ready to pluck you clean. Your emotions are running the show, and that spells L-O-S-E.

Capital Allocation

Give yourself a chance to win. Allocate your trading capital over a series of campaigns, each containing a fixed number of trade opportunities. This, too, needs to be realistic and in conformity with your trading profile. Don't expect to have 30 opportunities to make 100-pip profits with a $300 mini account.

If the math and ratio calculations are confusing at this point but you are itching to trade, don't panic. You can allocate your capital in advance in fixed proportions and at least not hurt yourself too badly. I am grateful to Bruce Gould, world-renowned futures trader, for this basic concept. His *Bruce Gould On Commodities* offers a plethora of commonsense money management ideas (www.brucegould.com).

Allocate your capital into two or three campaigns of 10 trades each.

- If you are a guerilla, set a 2:1 profit objective to stop-loss.
- If you are a scalper, set a 3:1 profit objective to stop-loss.
- If you are a day trader, set a 5:1 objective to stop-loss.

I do *not* recommend beginning traders attempt the position trader profile.

Summary

This is just a broad-strokes look at money management to introduce the key ideas and get you thinking in risk-avoidance mode. The key elements are your trading profile and matching it to the three money management ratios discussed here. I build on these basic elements in detail in Parts 2 and 3 of *GSIFTS*.

Part

Developing a Trading Codex

4

The Codex Notebook

You learn more from your losses than from your wins.
—Charles B. Goodman

I t is time to begin thinking in codex process terms and developing your own personal trading codex. In this book I use my own FxCodex approach as the example, but each trader will develop a codex according to his propensities and decisions with respect to trading techniques, style, and money management.

The first step is to begin a codex notebook. This is where you will keep all your trading parameters as well as copies of your daily and weekly trading reports and post-trade comments. In the remaining chapters of Part Two, I define the codex trader and help you assemble everything needed to trade using the codex approach.

From Traditional to Codex

Five key elements separate the traditional approach and the codex approach:

1. The trading elements of techniques, style, and money management are wrapped into an integrated, dynamic process instead of each element being considered separately from the others, one after the other in linear fashion.
2. Your codex is defined in advance of your trading. It may and will change from time to time, but the basic framework should be in place from the very beginning of your trading career.

3. Your perspective toward markets is in seeking trading opportunities, first qualifying them as candidates and then moving gradually to executing an actual trade. The elements are subordinate to that process.

4. Changes to your codex—your comprehensive trading approach—should be made in small evolutionary moves derived from trading results and experience. Avoid major and frequent changes.

5. You will constantly review your trading performance in light of your codex.

Elements versus Codex Approach

Elements
- Trading tools
- Style
- Money management

Codex
- Selection
- Entry
- Monitor
- Exit
- Postmortem

One student told me she considers process as the fourth element, after trading technique, soft elements, and money management. If you are a neotraditionalist, perhaps this is a good way to organize codex materials.

Codex Notebook

You are encouraged to begin a notebook to keep a written record of your codex selections and decisions. Later you will add a section for record keeping, including a daily and weekly trade plan.

You should keep your codex notebook with you at all times. You may want to keep a computer-based copy of it, but I strongly recommend maintaining a hard copy next to your computer whenever you trade or even watch the markets. The very act of writing things down, instead of putting them in a computer document, can make them more meaningful to you. You will want to keep records of all your trades in some fashion and in enough detail so that you can refer to them months later and remember most of the circumstances surrounding them. You also will want a daily and a weekly game plan—your analysis of ongoing and potential trades, and proposed actions you will take given different market circumstances.

You should create five sections: Trading Tools, Style, Money Management, Process, and Reports. If, after you look at the report examples in Part Four, these seem too onerous, you may replace them with a shorter diary.

The Codex Notebook—Sections

Some traders keep extensive commentary, others only shorthand notes. Whichever works for you is best. The primary idea is to be able to remember and reconstruct a trade and the conditions surrounding it at a later time.

1. *Trade summary.* This should include entry and exit dates, price in/price out, and net profit in both pips and dollars. Leave two or three additional columns for calculating cumulative results later.

2. *Daily trade plan.* This should include contingencies for as many price occurrences as possible. If the market moves higher, if the market moves lower; if the market opens higher then falls, if the market opens lower than rises; if Market Environment factors, especially directional movement and volatility, change dramatically; what news or announcements are pending and how the market reacts to them.

3. *Daily and weekly trade summary.* Provide enough information to reconstruct the trade(s) and the conditions surrounding it at a later date.

4. *Codex summary.* Keep a record of all the trades you are watching or trading.

5. *Diary.* A diary allows you to summarize your trading day—the good, the bad, and the ugly. It is here that you want to rate your emotions going into the session and again coming out of the session.

Trading Tools

In the codex approach, trading tools are used to select candidate trades. In this section of your notebook, you will monitor candidates until they either disqualify themselves or become legitimate trading opportunities. The same tools are then used to execute the trade, monitor the trade, and exit the trade.

Trading Tools Checklist

As you enter a trade, check off your trading tools to make sure you have considered them all in your selection process. You may keep this as a separate notebook entry or in your daily trade plan. If you haven't considered a particular tool, why not? Altering the process without a very good reason is not recommended.

- Bar chart
- Swing chart
- GSCS
- Nofri
- Indicator 1
- Indicator 2
- Market environment ratings
- Filters

Style

Here you will define your soft elements. The soft elements refer to things not objectively quantifiable, such as psychology and attitude. A trading profile may also fit into the soft category. Every trader must make adjustments from time to time. The markets ebb, flow, shift, and change—and so do we. But over the long haul, these changes occur gradually and should not require wholesale alterations to your codex or your trading.

Soft Elements Checklist

Keep a list of your soft elements, refer to it for each trade, and keep a record of those elements for each completed trade.

The two most critical questions to ask here are:

1. Does the trade match your trader profile—guerilla, scalper, day trader, position trader?
2. How do the market environment factors for each trade (directional movement, volatility, thickness, and rhythm) match up vis-à-vis performance?

By reviewing a few dozen trades for market environment you will see what ME profiles work best for you—and what profiles to avoid.

Money Management

In the codex approach, money management decisions derive from your soft-element decisions and the trading tools selections. Very little is done with ad hoc rules, as is typical in the traditional approach to trading.

After you define your trading profile, it is possible to create simple risk-reward tables to see how a prospective opportunity shapes up vis-à-vis your profile.

Money Management Checklist

For each trade, keep in a log:

- Your intended risk/reward (stop/profit objective) levels. If you don't know these in advance, *don't make the trade!*

- Your intended stop/profit objective method: system, fixed ratio, support/resistance. I strongly recommend the fixed ratio method for new traders, moving to the system (Goodman) method after at least three trading campaigns of 10 trades each. I recommend against the support/resistance method. Both broker/dealers and professional traders gun for stops in common support/resistance price levels.

- Your *intended* entry/exit versus the actual entry/exit.

Process

In your notebook, create a fourth section for codex process. Your codex summary should indicate where in the process each of your trades and trade candidates are at the beginning and the end of each session: select (candidate), entry, monitor, exit, or debrief (postmortem).

For trades in the *monitor* area, it is critical you have your daily trade plan tied in to any and all markets.

Reports or Diary

The fifth section is for reports or a diary. This section must include the basic details of each trade: when you entered, when you exited, prices, and time. Even a one-sentence comment on the trade—what went right or wrong, what seemed to work or not work—is useful. Write enough so you can recall the circumstances of the trade later.

Summary

Your notebook is designed to allow you to review past trades you have completed, keep track of ongoing trades, and prepare for future trades. There is obviously much flexibility in how you organize this information, but those are the three primary goals of a notebook.

Now it's time to begin the real work of building your personal trading codex.

Chapter 5

The Codex Toolbox

Keep it simple, Dad!

—Charles B. Goodman

art Two introduces the tools and other methods you will use for your personal codex. In Part Three, I show how they are utilized in the process of tracking, selecting, entering, monitoring, and exiting an actual trade.

The tools I use for trading are simple and transparent. They can be used effectively by traders of all profiles and in any FOREX market. The markets can only go up or down; everything beyond that simple fact should be irrelevant to the codex trader.

Trading is a simple business; do not make it unnecessarily complicated. The more complicated your trading techniques, the more difficult it is to find good trades, make trades, and diagnose problems.

The codex trader seeks only trades meeting the criteria within all three elements of the toolbox, the trader's style, and money management. Because there are so many markets to trade, it makes good sense to be picky. Most of the money you make will come from "sitting on your hands." If you select your codex materials correctly, it is easy to find good trades. You will have done much of the work in advance and the markets will receive your full concentration.

Trading Techniques—The Codes Toolbox

For trading, the only tools you need are the following:

- A tool to quickly define what type of market you are studying.
- A tool to visually observe market action.

67

- A tool to zero in on a market when a promising opportunity arises.
- A tool to forecast the market for determining entry and exit.

I emphasize again the danger of using too many different tools to trade. The markets are not that complicated, nor is any magic involved. Use as few tools as possible, and use only tools that are inherently transparent and easy to use, understand, and apply. See Figure 5.1.

Market Environment

I devised the market environments approach in the 1980s and have used it consistently since that time. It is a simple and useful method for quickly determining what type of market you are trading or considering to trade. Using market environments, you can also quickly and easily see if a market's underlying structure is changing.

There are four components to a market environment. Taking them together I call *eyeballing* a market. I believe you can learn more about a market in this manner than with a large variety of complex indicators. You can see all

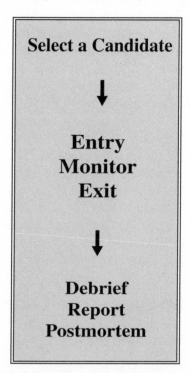

FIGURE 5.1 The Codex Approach.

of them simply by looking at a bar chart. Gaining information about a market from a chart is always preferable to secondary methods such as indicators.

Every market you trade may be defined in terms of directional movement and volatility (DM/V). These are the two primary components of market environment and eyeballing a trade.

Directional Movement and Volatility

Directional movement (DM) is the net change in prices over a specified number of time units. *Volatility* (V) is the aggregate price movement over a specified number of time units given a minimum measured price fluctuation.

EUR/USD Weekly Average Price
117.5
116.9
117.7
118.0
117.4
117.5
117.0
118.1
DM = .9
V = 4.3

The volatility number (4.3) is a raw value and is typically used as the variable to compute a volatility index or moving average.

Directional movement is the net price change over some period of time. *Volatility* is how much price movement occurs in addition to the straight line of directional movement. The former denotes the basic trend of a market; the latter, how actively it is trading.

I use a simple computer program for market environment that creates a 16-combination matrix of directional movement and volatility. It shows a continuum going from low directional movement and low volatility to high directional movement and high volatility. You can also subdivide according to whether the basic market trend is up or down. This, then, gives 32 possible market environments. Eyeballing is almost as good. After you have studied some charts, you can get a good estimate of both factors and where a market lies on the continuum.

The basic market environment uses these two features of prices—directional movement and volatility. As stated earlier, directional movement is

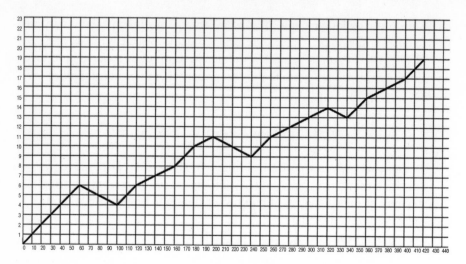

FIGURE 5.2   15-Minute Directional Movement.

the net price change from one time unit to another. Volatility is the gross price movement between those two points. See Figures 5.2 and 5.3.

The Visual Basic 6 code in Appendix A will allow you to work with market environments more precisely, should you want to do so. If you are unable to use the code, you can simply eyeball the chart you are watching for the two factors of directional movement and volatility. Also watch for changes in both factors as prices develop. You can visually plot the movement of a market on the DM/V scale as it evolves over time.

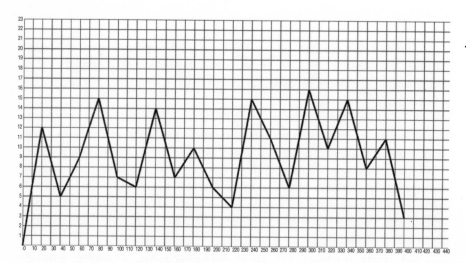

FIGURE 5.3   15-Minute Volatility.

The Market Environment Continuum

Directional movement can be valued on a continuum from 1 to 10, where 1 is the lowest DM in the data sample and 10 is the highest. A similar continuum may be used for volatility.

A 1-1 market exhibits low DM and low V. A 10-10 market exhibits high DM and high V.

Secondary Market Environment Factors

Thickness is the third market environment factor. Thickness refers to how much overlay there is in prices from high to low from one time unit to the next. (See Figure 5.4.) Some FOREX pairs seem to be naturally thick. Thick markets tend to trade more slowly, even sluggishly. As a practitioner of the Belgian Dentist style of trading, thick markets appeal to me. In Europe, the term *Belgian Dentist* is used to refer to the most ultraconservative of traders.

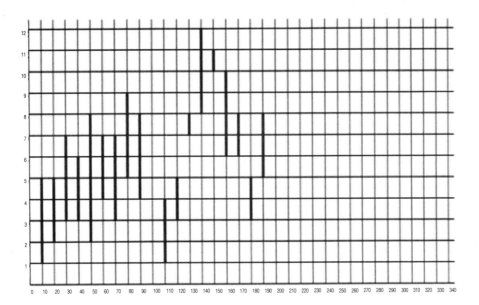

FIGURE 5.4 Thickness.

Thickness measures how much of the price value, from high to low, for a given time unit (X), is used in the next time unit (X+1). The market on the left is thick, and the market on the right is thin. Thin markets tend to have higher directional movements, but it is not always the case.

A note of caution: Thickness may also indicate that a pair is relatively illiquid. That is, there is not a great volume of trading involved and the thickness actually represents a wide bid-ask spread.

In Part One I wrote about cyclical analysis. I've long ago concluded that the markets do have some natural rhythms and cycles, which would be an excellent avenue for further technical analysis exploration. Surprisingly little has been done in this field, especially regarding FOREX.

But you don't need software or complex indicators to get an overview of a market's *rhythm*, which is the fourth basic component of market environments. Simply observe the following:

- The lengths of the upswings in a market and the corresponding lengths of the downswings.
- The time between peaks and valleys, peaks and peaks, and valleys and valleys.

You want to trade with the market's rhythm, not against it. If a market is having fairly regular 200-pip upswings and 100-pip downswings, you don't want to enter a sell order after a 50-pip upswing unless you have overwhelming evidence to the contrary.

Most markets exhibit some rhythm. Rhythm may be either time-based, meaning the units of time from peak to peak and valley to valley are regular, or price-based, meaning primary and secondary price swings are regular.

Keep a mental or written notation of average rhythm. Rhythms do change but they tend to change gradually and predictably.

Rhythm can be used to time market entry and exit (see Figure 5.5).

These, then, are the four components of market environments. I truly believe you can be a successful trader by simply learning, refining, and using these factors.

Bar Charts

The best chart to use for studying market environments is the bar chart. Bar charts are also the best backbone tool a trader can use, although the traditional interpretation patterns such as pennants and head-and-shoulders are essentially worthless nowadays.

Price charts are simply visual records of price movements. They allow you to see prices over an extended period of time. Each type of chart—bar, point and figure, candlestick, and swing—has its own specific characteristics and advantages. But they all perform primarily as recording devices.

Bar charts are the most popular. They are widely used on FOREX broker/dealer trading platforms and are the most commonly used and discussed in

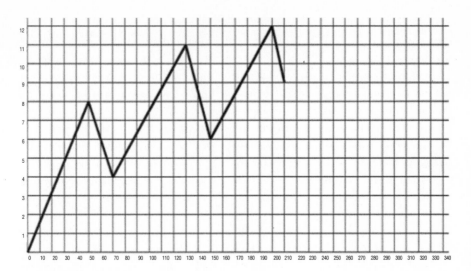

FIGURE 5.5 Rhythm.
This market has both time and price rhythm. Watch for both types of rhythm, and rhythm for peaks/primary-valleys/secondary (in up markets) and valleys/primary-peaks/secondary (in down markets). Watch for rhythm in all three of your chart price scales.

the literature of the market. Candlesticks are second in popularity, with point and figure and swing charts a distant third and fourth.

A single vertical bar on a bar chart represents the range of prices for a specified period of time, from the highest price during that time period to the lowest price.

Charlie always said, "Keep it simple," but he could just as well have said, "Keep it visual." To be close to the market's pulse, you need tools directly derived from market data; in the case of FOREX, that means prices.

Volume and Open Interest

Futures and option traders use volume and open interest figures to analyze markets. Volume is a continued total number of futures option contracts that have traded during a specified trading session. Open interest is the number of futures or option contracts open at any given time.

Because there is no central clearinghouse for FOREX, currency traders do not have access to these useful tools. It is possible to synthesize volume and open interest using price data. See the FOREX Propensity Index on www.fxpraxis.com.

Each time data is translated—for example, to create an indicator—it becomes more difficult to use. Each translation or conversion also tends to lower the clarity of the information. We all know what happens when a picture or graphic is copied and then the copy is copied again. It loses resolution and eventually you cannot recognize the image itself. The same is true of data generally and market data specifically. See Figure 5.6.

Bar charts typically now indicate the opening price for that time period as well as the closing price. These are represented by small horizontal dashes attached to the main vertical bar. See Figure 5.7.

The time period selected for a bar chart may vary enormously. In FOREX, bar charts may be used for time frames of seconds (5, 10, 30), minutes (1, 5, 10, 30), or even days or weeks. Most broker-dealer trading platforms offer a wide variety of time frames. Properly used, these can be an enormous benefit to the FOREX trader. (See Figure 5.8.) The time period(s) you select for your codex will be determined by your trader profile. The shorter term you trade, the shorter term will be the time frames of your bar charts.

FIGURE 5.6 A Bar Chart.
A bar chart connects the high to the low price on a specified time unit. Bar charts may be used with any time unit from five seconds to monthly or even yearly. Most bar charts add a small horizontal bar to indicate closing and sometimes opening prices.

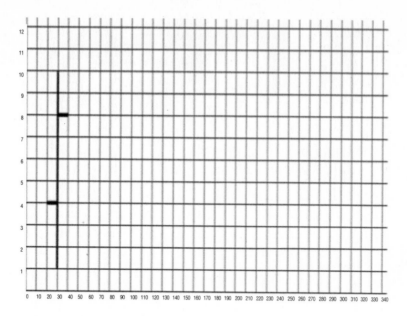

FIGURE 5.7 A Completed Bar.
Many traders find value in the relative locations of all four values: high, low, open, and close. The relationship between open and close is especially well scrutinized, and a variety of indicators have been designed to analyze their relative values.

Bar charts, point and figure charts, and swing charts are all *refractive*. This means that without seeing the time and price legends, it is impossible to tell a five-minute chart from a weekly chart in most cases. The useful corollary of this is that trading techniques used on one time frame can be used on all others. This is an important feature of technical analysis and also of great value to the FOREX trader.

Popular Bar Chart Patterns

Traditional bar-chart interpretation looks for specific formations within the chart. There are many so-called patterns, but the following are the ones most commonly watched for and used. For more information, see *Encyclopedia of Chart Patterns* by Thomas Bulkowski (New York: Wiley Trading, Second Ed., 2005).

- Head and shoulders
- Pennant
- Flag
- Double bottom/double top
- V-top/V-bottom

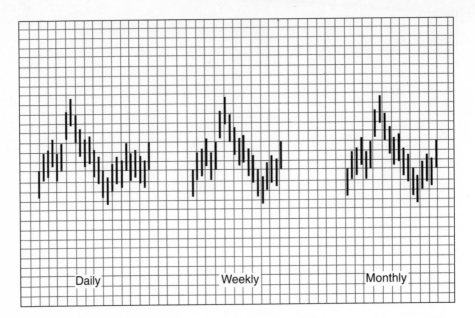

FIGURE 5.8 Time Frames.

Time frames, or time scales, are a very valuable tool to the currency trader. Each gives a different perspective on a market, and the relationships between the frames are useful. Typically you will select markets off the middle frame, and use the larger frame for long-term perspective and the smaller from for entry and exit timing.

I do not recommend trading using these patterns as they are too popular and the market tends to anticipate them, which prevents them from working very well. It is useful to watch for them if only to know what many other traders might do in reaction to them.

These patterns are very well known because they have been popularized over many years in many books and other market instruction. For this reason I do not believe they are effective over the longer term. You may certainly find one that works according to plan, but for each one that works, several will fail. As an example, see Figure 5.9.

Traditional bar-chart patterns also tend to be backward-looking, and the markets are always forward-looking. If you look at a bar chart, you will easily see many of these patterns after the fact, after they have been completed. Those won't help you make a successful trade; it's too late! Keep in mind the difference between a tool being descriptive or predictive. A descriptive tool is not much use unless you have a time machine.

Figure 5.10 shows a bar chart pattern. But hold a piece of paper over the chart and then move it one time frame at a time to the right (as prices progress). At what point would you execute a trade based on the pattern visible so far? Remember, you haven't seen the entire pattern because it hasn't yet formed.

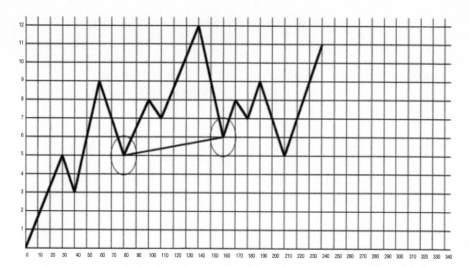

FIGURE 5.9 Failure of a Bar Chart Formation.
The two circled points connected by the horizontal sloped line is the "neckline" of a head and shoulders formation. According to the theory, once the neckline is broken by downward-moving prices, a sharp downward trend will continue. Often, however, prices will break the neckline, only to head back up.

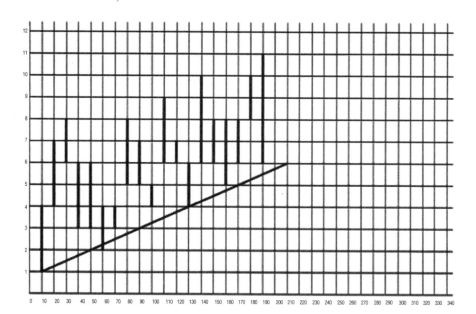

FIGURE 5.10 Descriptive or Predictive?
This trend line appears to be very tradable. But was it predictive or simply descriptive?

If you review a large number of charts you will see many head and shoulders formations that worked. The problem is these patterns tend to be descriptive rather than predictive. To accurately measure reliability cover a chart with a plain piece of paper, then move it one frame at a time and attempt to predict a head and shoulders. Your results will differ substantially! Beware of tools that are descriptive (you can see them work after the fact) but are not predictive.

The codex approach does not use these patterns, but it is useful to be able to recognize them. In Part Three I show you how the codex trader uses them to their greatest effectiveness.

Another issue with traditional patterns is that because so many traders follow them, they simply cannot work. The market will not let them work or else everyone would win, which is impossible.

I once acted as an expert on an Internet FOREX forum. The moderator gave me the boot because my ideas about chart patterns were not mainstream. But mainstream doesn't win in the markets—stocks, futures, *or* FOREX.

In the old days, traders created their own bar charts by hand. This was very time consuming but it also had advantages. The very act of making the chart helped the trader tune in to the markets. Because you will be trading multiple markets with very short time frames this is, unfortunately, a luxury no longer affordable.

Bathtub Analysis

My mentor, Charles B. Goodman, used what he called *bathtub analysis*. He would take a book of charts into the bath and analyze them. By *analyze* he meant asking questions, making hypotheses, and testing them. If you don't look for something, you can rarely find it. On the other hand, if you test for even the wildest hypotheses you will often find yourself hot on the trail of something very useful.

Be sure to cover charts with a plain piece of paper and move it slowly to the right to duplicate the market as it happened.

All the major FOREX broker/dealer trading platforms offer customizable bar charts. You can keep multiple charts on multiple pairs with multiple time frames! This advantage easily surpasses any to be had from drawing your own charts. Most of the charts in this book are from the Intellicharts FxTrek service, www.fxtrek.com.

Swing Charts

Swing charts were first popularized by Burton Pugh in his 1933 book, *The Great Wheat Secret*. When I traded commodities, I used swing charts almost exclusively. Unfortunately, today they are not popular, so you will need to keep your own if you decide to use them. If not, point and figure charts, more readily available online, can be used as a satisfactory substitute.

The codex approach in general, and the Goodman Swing Count System (GSCS) specifically, both rely heavily on price swings, especially for timing entry and exit. The Goodman Swing Count System is the backbone of my trading method, FxCodex, and is detailed later in this chapter.

Whereas bar charts are time-specific—that is, each unit is a unit of time—most swing charts are price-specific (see Figure 5.11). Drawing them depends not on the passage of some fixed time frame, but on the movement of a fixed price range. Point and figure charts are also price-specific. A price-specific chart requires a minimum price increment to build. A time-specific chart requires a specific time unit to build.

Just as you must select the time frame for a bar chart, you must select a price unit for a swing or point and figure chart. The smaller your price unit, the more detail the chart will display. Larger price units filter out the smaller movements. Such decisions will depend on what trader profile you select. See Figures 5.12 and 5.13.

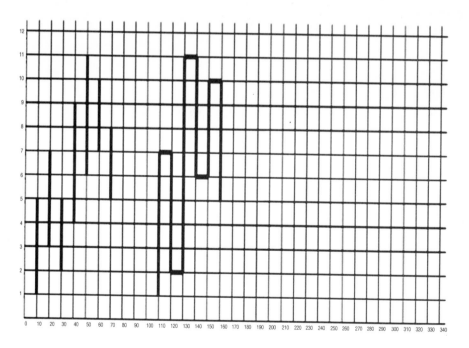

FIGURE 5.11 Time- versus Price-Specific Charts.
The bar chart on the left is time-specific; bars are drawn in accordance with specific time units. The swing chart on the right is price-specific; swings are drawn only in accordance with specific price changes.

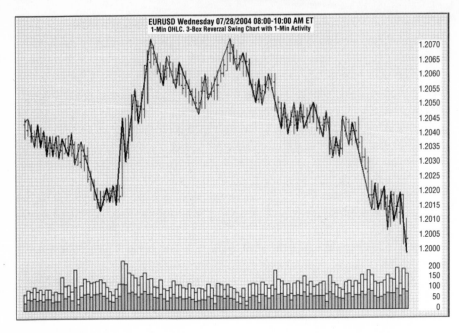

FIGURE 5.12   A Swing Chart.

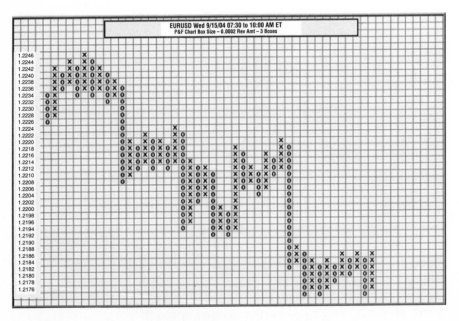

FIGURE 5.13   A Point and Figure Chart.

The rules for drawing a swing chart are simple:

1. Select the minimum price reversal unit. This will be the minimum length of any vertical swing.

2. Draw your first line *up* if prices are going higher, or *down* if prices are going lower. The first line must be at least 100 percent of the value of your price reversal unit.

3. Keep extending the line as long as prices move in that direction in any additional amount.

4. As soon as the price reverses (down from up, or up from down) by the value of your minimum price reversal, draw a small horizontal line and begin a second vertical line in the opposite direction.

5. Repeat steps 3 and 4.

Drawing a Swing Chart

1. Determine a minimum price fluctuation.

2. Draw the first trend (vertical line) in the same direction until prices move in the opposite direction by your minimum price fluctuation or more.

3. Connect this trend to the next trend with a horizontal line over the distance of one graph grid.

4. Draw the second trend (vertical line) in the same direction until prices move in the opposite direction (the first trend) by your minimum price fluctuation or more.

5. Continue steps 3 and 4.

My mentor, Charles B. Goodman, developed a time-specific swing chart. These are not available on any broker/dealer trading platform, so if they appeal to you, it's necessary for you to keep your own. In honor of Charlie, I call them CG charts.

The CG swing chart begins with a small horizontal bar for the opening price. You must know whether prices for a time period first went up or first went down. The first vertical line depicts this action. It is connected to a second horizontal line. The second vertical line depicts the opposite movement for that time period. A final horizontal line is drawn to show the last or closing price for that time period. See Figure 5.14.

I show you how to interpret and use swing charts in Part Three. I use bar charts for most steps of the trade selection process and swing charts for entry and exit.

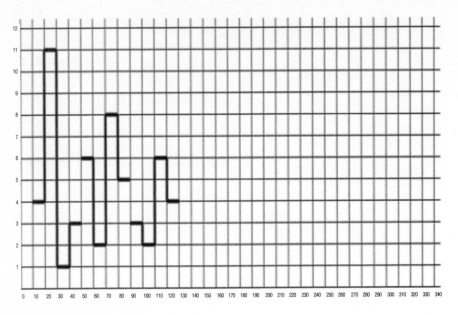

FIGURE 5.14 CG Charts.

I recommend using a red horizontal line for the opening price and a green horizontal line for the closing price.

Drawing a CG Chart

1. Use a horizontal bar for the opening.

2. Draw a vertical line to either the high or the low for the time unit, whichever occurred first.

3. Connect the first trend to the second trend with a horizontal line.

4. Draw a vertical line to the low or the high, whichever occurred last.

5. Connect the second trend with the closing line with a horizontal line.

6. Draw a vertical line to the close.

7. Note the close with a horizontal line.

Goodman Swing Count System

I learned this chart interpretation from Charles B. Goodman in the early 1970s. Throughout the intervening years, I have continued to find it the best method for reading charts. It is simple, logical, and transparent. The basics can be learned and applied quickly, but deep study is also possible.

I believe the Goodman Swing Count System (GSCS) to be a vast improvement over both Gann and Elliott. It is certainly more logical and easy to apply. It also offers more predictive opportunities than either Gann or Elliott, which seem to me to be primarily descriptive in nature.

The Goodman Swing Count System makes use of the refractive nature of price charts. Price charts in FOREX and other markets follow the same rules whether they detail a very short-term history (tick charts) or a very long-term history (monthly charts). Given a set of charts of different price histories, without a scale it is usually difficult to tell which is a short-term record and which is a long-term record.

This brief tutorial provides only an overview of GSCS and enough information to trade the easiest-to-recognize Goodman patterns. If you have further interest in GSCS, you can visit my web site, www.fxpraxis.com, or refer to my book *The FOREX Chartist Companion*.

GSCS Components

There are three components to a Goodman chart: a trend or swing, a matrix, and a Goodman Wave. Swings build into matrices and matrices build into waves. A Goodman Wave is a completed set of five swings of price; one matrix becomes a component of a larger matrix—the wave.

Trend

A trend is a price movement over some period of time without a significant correction (a price move in the direction opposite the trend). The operative word here is *significant*. In Goodman, corrections of 25 percent of the trend or less are seldom significant.

In GSCS, a trend is called a swing. See Figure 5.15.

Fifty Percent Move and Measured Move

The cornerstone of GSCS is the old "50 percent retracement and measured move" rule. This rule, familiar to most traders, is almost as old as the organized markets themselves. It has been traced to the times when insiders manipulated railroad stocks in the nineteenth century. See Figure 5.16.

The first systematic description of the 50 percent rule was given in Burton Pugh's *The Great Wheat Secret*, originally published in 1933. In 1973, Charles L. Lindsay published *Trident*. This book did much (some say too much!) to quantify and mathematically describe the 50 percent rule. Nevertheless, it is must reading for anyone interested in this area of market methodology. Edward L. Dobson wrote *The Trading Rule That Can Make You Rich* in 1978.

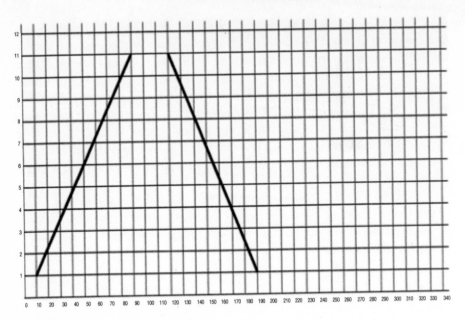

FIGURE 5.15 A Trend or Swing.
In GSCS a trend or swing is simply a price movement in one direction with less than a 25 percent correction.

This is a good work with some nice examples. But none of these, in my opinion, even scratch the surface relative to Goodman's work.

The logic of the 50 percent rule is quite simple. At a 50 percent retracement, both buyers and sellers of the previous trend (up or down) are, ceteris paribus, in balance. Half of each holds profits and half of each holds losses. See Figure 5.17.

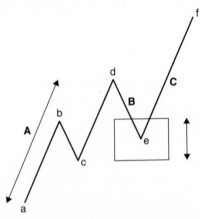

FIGURE 5.16 The 50 Percent Retracement and Measured Move Rule.
This is one of the oldest trading ideas but still one of the best. The example shown here is a Goodman Wave. In the author's opinion it is the most tradable pattern in all of the markets.

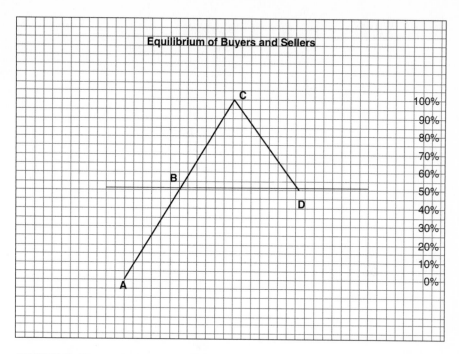

FIGURE 5.17 A Market Tug of War.
The 50 percent retracement is the price area to watch! It represents the point or area where buyers and sellers of the primary trend are in aggregate equilibrium.

This equilibrium is a tenuous one, indeed. The distribution of buyers and sellers over the initial price trend or *swing* is not perfectly even: Some buyers hold more contracts than other buyers. They also have different propensities for taking profits or losses. Nor does it account for the buyers and sellers who have entered the market before the initial swing or during the reaction swing. Not all of the buyers and sellers from the original swing may be in the market any longer.

Remarkably, GCSC eventually takes all of this into account—especially the buyers and sellers at other price swing levels, called *matrices.*

Nevertheless, the 50 percent retracement point is often a powerful and very real point of equilibrium and certainly a known and defined hot spot of which the trader should be aware. Remember that both the futures markets and the currency markets are very close to a zero-sum game. It is only commissions, pips, and slippage that keep them from being zero-sum. At the 50 percent point, it doesn't take much to shift the balance of power for that particular swing matrix.

The 50 percent rule also states that the final (third) swing of the move—back in the direction of the initial swing—will equal the value of the initial swing. The logic of this idea, called the *measured move,* is seen in Figure 5.18.

As I have indicated, examples of the 50 percent rule occur at *all* price levels or matrices, and many are being worked simultaneously in any given

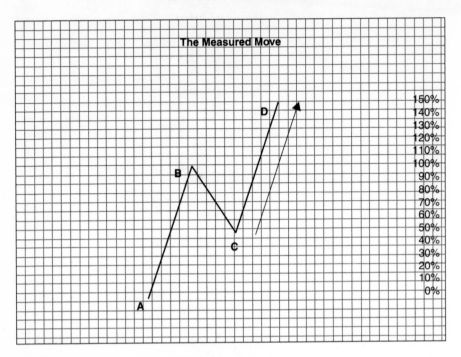

FIGURE 5.18 The Measured Move—A Matrix.
A matrix is the 3-wing measured move. It is *not* a Goodman Wave, which comprises five swings.

ongoing market. This refractive behavior is a critical point. Simply stated, this means that without labeling, you could not really tell the difference between a 10-minute chart and a daily or weekly chart. They all exhibit the same behavior and operate under the same principles.

Wave Generation

After a measured move is completed, it becomes a matrix, the beginning of a larger measured move with this matrix as the first swing. The completed price record of a matrix built into a larger matrix is a Goodman Wave. See Figure 5.19.

Elliott versus GSCS   For Elliott, a wave is composed of three components; for Goodman, five components. See Figure 5.20.

The Return

In GSCS the return swing is the most critical part of the entire wave. See Figure 5.21.

The 4-swing in the propagation of a Goodman Wave is the return wave. This is the wave that converts the first matrix into a single swing component of

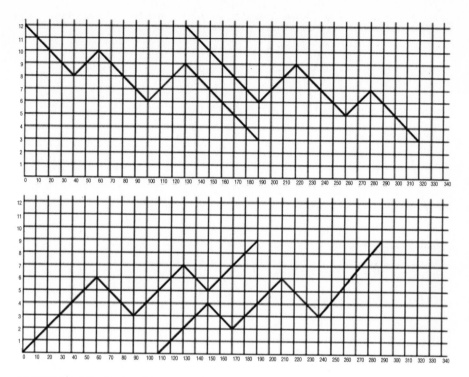

FIGURE 5.19 Swing Matrix and Goodman Wave.
A Goodman Wave is a matrix taken as swing 1 as a component of a larger matrix. The 5-swing matrix is a Goodman Wave. The 4-swing is the critical *return swing*.

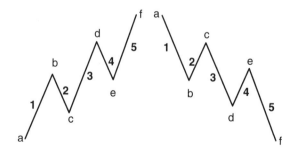

FIGURE 5.20 Goodman versus Elliott.
In Elliott Wave theory the 4-swing is a non-unique component of the 5-swing Elliott Wave. In GSCS the 4-swing is a unique component that propagates the first matrix into a Goodman Wave.

a Goodman Wave. If the 50 percent return of a matrix represents equilibrium of all traders in the 1-swing, the return represents equilibrium of all traders in the 1-2-3-swing matrix. Trading off the return is one of the three easiest and most reliable GSCS trades.

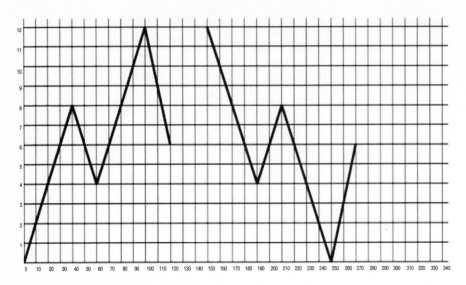

FIGURE 5.21   The Return Swing.

Flat and Complex Rule

According to Goodman, if the first matrix is flat (a single swing), the second matrix will be complex, composed of three swings. If the first matrix is complex, the second matrix will be flat. This rule is extremely useful in anticipating the propagation of a Goodman Wave. (It is probably also why Elliott missed the fact that the 4-swing is a critical return swing and not just a non-unique component of a 1-2-3-4-5 swing.) Trading by anticipating the propagation of a Goodman Wave is the second of the three most useful GSCS trading patterns. See Figure 5.22.

The return and the flat/complex rule provide excellent trading opportunities.

Advanced Goodman Rules

There is much more to GSCS theory; a complete set of ordinal and cardinal rules can be applied. *Ordinal* rules refer to chart formations only, with no reference to specific prices or price measurements. *Cardinal* rules reference specific price values and calculations. Previously, I have shown the ordinal rules. Following is a brief introduction to the cardinal rules.

Intersection

Intersection is the most important and most interesting cardinal rule in GSCS. It refers to areas of price and time where two waves or matrices using the 50

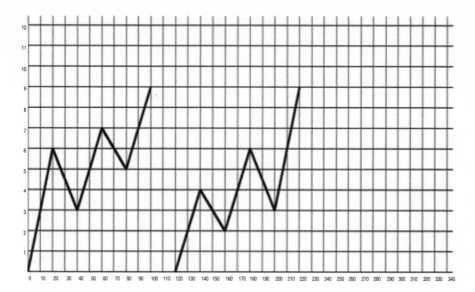

FIGURE 5.22 The Flat/Complex Rule.
If the first component of a Goodman Wave is simple (a single swing) the
second component will usually be complex (a 1-2-3 swing or matrix). If the
first component of a Goodman Wave is complex, the second component will
usually be simple.

percent rule and measured move intersect. These are extremely reliable areas of
support and resistance, and it is useful to trade against these points or areas.

The double intersection is the third and most reliable (but most difficult
to find) of the three basic Goodman trading patterns, the first two being the return swing and trading wave propagation. See Figure 5.23.

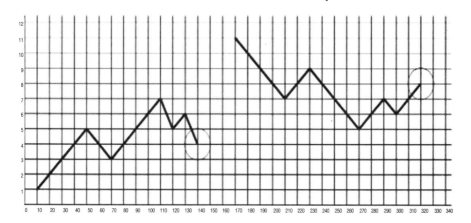

FIGURE 5.23 Double Intersection.

There are several forms of double intersection. The most common is the 50 percent return of a matrix being the measured move of another matrix. The double intersection represents equilibrium at three points.

The triple intersection is an advanced GSCS pattern. I do not recommend attempting to find it or use it until you have mastered the three basic patterns. (See Figure 5.24.) Traders should first learn to see and anticipate wave propagations, returns, and double intersections without regard to measurement (ordinal). After mastering those tasks, learn the cardinal measurement rules.

Cancellation and Carryover

Often prices do not exactly hit the 50 percent retracement. The Goodman Swing Count System states that whatever amount a matrix is short of or over the 50 percent measurement, it will eventually make up in a subsequent matrix. The ± value is carried over until it cancels and equals zero. See Figures 5.25 and 5.26.

Brackets and Points

Brackets refer to price areas where different price matrices intersect. See Figure 5.27. The brackets were a great mystery to traders when Charlie made them on

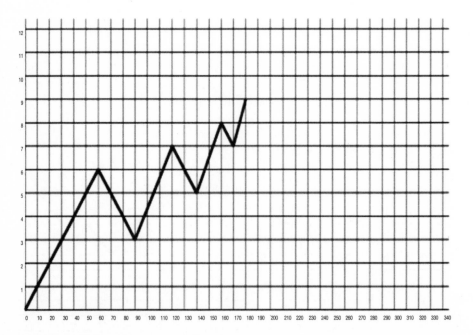

FIGURE 5.24 Triple Intersection.
The triple intersection represents equilibrium at four points.

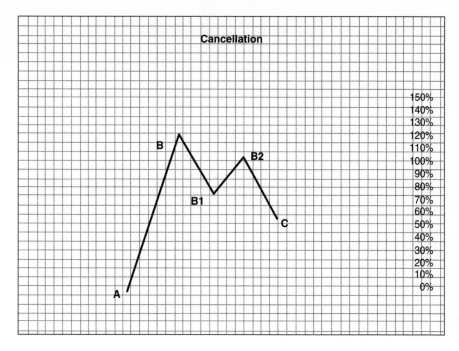

FIGURE 5.25 Cancellation.

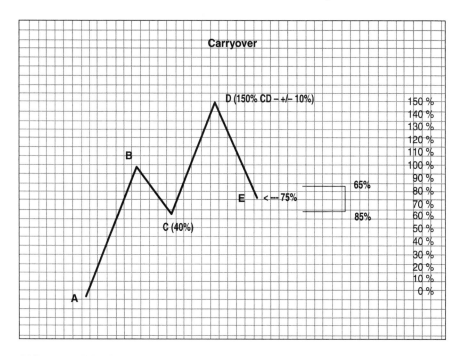

FIGURE 5.26 Carryover.

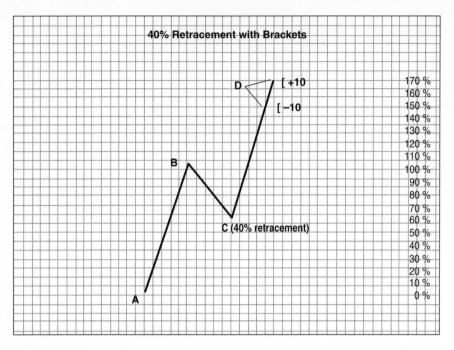

FIGURE 5.27   Brackets.

the large wall charts at Peavey & Company. They essentially represent areas of anticipated intersections and measurements. You always paid attention when prices moved into areas where brackets overlapped.

There are five key points that may be defined relative to any swing. As the swing builds, these points will change. (See Figure 5.28.) The points of a swing from any initial swing can give the trader a rough idea of how and where a Goodman Wave may propagate. As possibilities are eliminated, one gets closer and closer to a trading candidate.

Trading GSCS

GSCS may be traded in a number of ways, from various patterns and rules. The following four trade formations are the easiest to spot.

  1. *The return.* This is the easiest pattern to trade. It may be traded with or without measurement rules. At the end of the 4-swing in a Goodman Wave, even if the wave ultimately does not form, a sharp tradable move is common in many markets. Trading off the return swing is idea for scalpers and day traders.

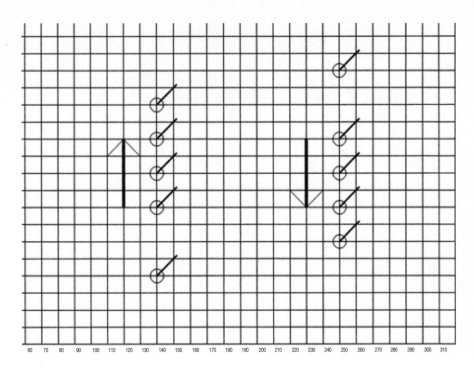

FIGURE 5.28 Points of a Swing.

2. *Flat/complex rule.* If the first swing is flat, you may anticipate the second swing in a Goodman Wave being complex and trade off the anticipated propagation of the complex swing. Guerillas may like this pattern since it occurs often on very small time frame charts.

3. *Double intersection.* This can be traded without measurements, but with measurements it is the finest single trading pattern available. Look for a sharp move in either direction off a double intersection. Remember, it represents equilibrium at the points. As the traders on the wrong side unwind their positions, prices can and often do move sharply.

4. *Wave propagation.* Anticipating a Goodman Wave may offer a number of trades over a period of time. It is best for day traders and position traders. If you get in sync with a wave you may ride it for several profitable trades. But when the music stops, don't fight it—move on. Use the five points of a Goodman Wave to initially map a wave.

There is much more to GSCS theory, including a notational calculus and a charting technique. But these four trade formations are enough to keep any trader busy for a long time. Even if you follow only a few markets at three different trading levels, you will find multiple strategic opportunities every trading day.

I could very well stop right here. With market environments and GSCS, you are already better armed to trade than most traders!

Goodman Cycle Count System

I offer this section as an extra for experts, for those who want to do some independent exploration and research. It is a Goodman system for time, in contrast to GSCS, which is for price. Either Charlie didn't have it fully developed or he simply didn't share the details with me. It took me 20 years after his passing (in 1984) to reconstruct it from a few charts he left that used it.

I use GSCS primarily and the Goodman Cycle Count System (GCCS) as only a check or overlay to confirm GSCS.

Charlie had a counting system for cycles (time) as well as prices. He never explained it to me in depth, but I know he used it. The time points would be overlaid on his price charts, I assume as a confirming type of signal.

Just as GSCS calculates price targets, GCCS calculates time targets. The union of these two targets is called a *landing area*.

Although I have hundreds of Charlie's price count charts, I was left only a half-dozen or so examples of the cycle count system. Through the years since his passing, I have taken those out on occasion and spent a few minutes looking at them, but until recently, I had never figured out the key to the cycle/time count system.

A few months ago I tried a new tack. It worked! As is often the case after figuring something out, I wondered, "How did I miss this before?" In the case of the cycle count, I had tried to make it more complex and less transparent than it was and had misconstrued Charlie's use of the word *cycle*. In this case, it is actually the same as a swing. After I grasped that concept, it was a matter of trying a few different measurement paradigms to figure out what Charlie was calculating to and from.

I'm not done researching GCCS—I plan to run an in-depth computer study of it soon—but I'm confident I have the basic key to it right now and so I am sharing it with you via the example in Figure 5.29. I hope you find this example interesting.

GCCS is identical to GSCS, except that instead of using the vertical (price) length of the swing components to determine a price objective, you use the horizontal (time) distance from trough to trough and from peak to peak of swing components to achieve a time objective.

The underlying logic is somewhat similar to GSCS. In GSCS the values of swing component 1 and swing component 2 determine the price objective for swing component 3. In GCCS, the trough-to-trough or peak-to-peak measurement of swing component 1 and the peak-to-peak or trough-to-trough measurement of swing component 2 determine the time objective for swing component 3.

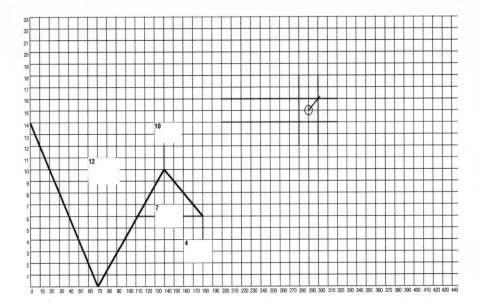

FIGURE 5.29 The Goodman Cycle Count System.

This is an important distinction between GSCS and GCCS: You need an extra (prior) swing component (called *0 swing*) to generate and/or calculate a GCCS time count.

Figure 5.29 displays the basic GCCS paradigm. If you are familiar with GSCS, perhaps you can work out the mapping to other Goodman ordinal and cardinal principles. If not, stay tuned!

For GCCS, measurements are taken from the peak of a swing component to the point horizontal with it on the previous swing component. The next measurement is taken from the most current point in the next swing component back horizontal to the first swing component. Just as in GSCS, the most current swing is in process, so measurements change with time and price.

If the first measurement is a primary swing and the next one is a secondary swing (as in Figure 5.29), the secondary swing cycle measurement should be one-half the primary swing measurement—in this instance, 6.

Here, the secondary measurement is 7. Calculation is as follows: The next primary swing will fall (in time) ± 1 from the ideal measurement point of 6 on the secondary swing measurement.

I've also calculated the GSCS price count for this wave. The union of the two boxes is the calculated landing area for the integrated price (GSCS) and time (GCCS) measurements.

Again, as the most current swing component builds, both calculations can change and, thus, the landing area.

I find this quite exciting—a technical analysis tool hidden for so many years. I'm currently working on GCCS intersection, carryover, and cancellation aspects; these appear to be slightly different from their GSCS concepts. There are also some special formations worth noting, and ordinal versus cardinal principles, as well.

Don't work with GCCS until you've mastered both the ordinal and cardinal rules of GSCS. I find GCCS works best as a check on GSCS and not as a trading method in and of itself. But if you have a strong opinion in favor of trading cycles, it may well reward further exploration. As new research on GCCS is complete it will be published on www.fxpraxis.com, so please check for updates.

Nofri's Congestion Phase

In 1975, a well-known Chicago grain floor trader, Eugene Nofri, published *The Congestion Phase System* (New York: Pageant-Poseidon Press Ltd.). This small but power-packed volume detailed a short-term trading method using simple but effective "congestion phases." Although not precisely a work on the 50 percent rule, it touched on some of Charlie's ideas from a different angle. Mr. Nofri was a corn trader, but the congestion phase system is applicable to FOREX at all trading levels. Other congestion phases identified by Mr. Nofri are in his book. See Figure 5.30.

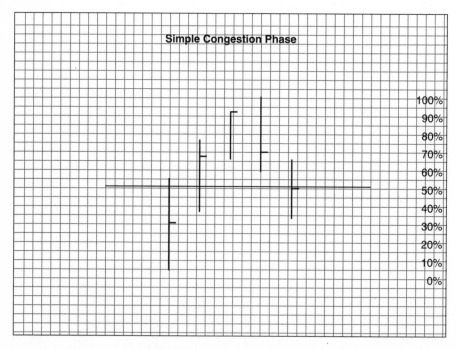

FIGURE 5.30 A Congestion Phase.

I mention Nofri's work also because Charlie was especially taken by its simplicity and because it can work well in conjunction with GCSC. The idea of melding GCSC with a congestion phase approach ought to produce a method of finding those high-percentage ducks that the Belgian Dentist loves so much.

Indicators

As I've written earlier, I am not a big fan of indicators. I think they are too far removed from the actual market data, which makes it difficult to reconnect them with fast-moving markets requiring instant decisions. Nor is it always easy to determine what they are actually measuring. You can't determine what you did wrong (or right) if you don't really know what you did! The visual clues using market environments offer a better approach.

Nevertheless, I do watch two very simple indicators. One of them is a simplified calculation of a market environment ratio; the other attempts to measure how important the price activity of any given period is to the broader scope of the market.

DM/V Ratio Indicator

This ratio will give you a quantified view of the relationship between directional movement and volatility for a market. It is also useful for observing how these two factors might be evolving for a particular market pair. The equation for calculating the DM/V ratio is as follows:

$$DMV = 100 \cdot \frac{DM}{V}$$

Impact Ratio Indicator

This is the ratio between the range of the open and close for a specific time frame and the full high to low range for that time. The theory is that the higher the ratio, the less critical the price action for that time period. If the ratio is low, it is assumed the price action for that time from high to low held more validity because it is closer to the open and close for that time period. See Figure 5.31.

The equation for calculating the impact ratio is:

$$Impact = 100 \yen \frac{Close - Open}{High - Low}$$

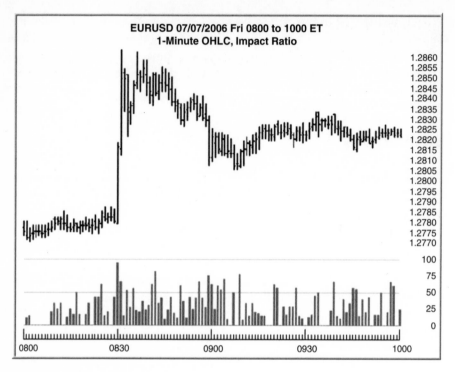

FIGURE 5.31   Impact Ratio.

Summary

With the exception of the Trend Machine, which is beyond the scope of this work, this is the entire set of tools I use for my own FxCodex trading. For information on the Trend Machine, refer to my web site, www.fxpraxis.com.

Don't worry if you are unclear on how to apply all these tools right now. The best way to learn how to use a tool is to use it. I show all of them in use in Parts Three and Four.

Remember, your money management techniques and trading style decisions are at least as important as your tool set.

I strongly advise against using more than five or six complementing trading tools. Beyond that number you are making the markets more complicated then they really are, and you will spend too much time just analyzing the markets. It is too easy to get confused. The confused trader is prone to letting his emotions take over, and that is not good.

FxCodex Toolbox

This is the toolbox, sans the Trend Machine, that I use to trade:

- Market environments and eyeballing
- Bar charts
- Swing charts
- GSCS
- Nofri
- DMV ratio
- Impact ratio

Your personal codex may contain all these tools, some of them, or none of them. You may want to substitute tools or add additional ones that have worked for you and that you are comfortable with. It is important that your tools complement each other, are easy to use, are transparent, and that you understand them thoroughly.

Keep it simple!

Chapter

Style

Style is a touchstone when you need to make a quick decision.
—Charles B. Goodman

Most FOREX traders never consciously develop a style. A specific style will assist you in determining what pairs and crosses to trade, which opportunities to pursue, and which to ignore. A style can be the touchstone allowing you to make a quick and accurate decision about a trade.

Of course, style evolves over time. You will find some of your initial selections and decisions to be incorrect in light of actual market experience. But making those selections before trading is still essential to the codex approach.

The Trader Profile

There are four primary trader profiles. These determine your market focus and help you select other style and money management parameters.

1. The guerilla trader.
2. The scalper.
3. The day trader.
4. The position trader.

Moving down the list, each type trades for successively bigger profits. Conversely, each trades less often.

I recommend the new trader focus on being either a scalper or a day trader. If you trade small positions as a guerilla. the pip spreads and ballooning spreads during news and announcements will make it difficult to succeed.

If you hold positions over several sessions as a position trader, you open your-self up to enormous risks, even if you use stops.

Each trader will use bar charts covering three distinct time frames or ranges. The middle-range chart is used to monitor the market on a per-session basis. The smaller range is used for timing entry and exit, and the largest is used to determine long-term trends and keep a perspective so that you don't lose the forest for the trees. See Figures 6.1, 6.2, and 6.3.

Trading Levels for Trader Profiles

Use the middle-range chart and prices for selecting candidate markets. Use the largest-range chart to gain a longer-term perspective. Use the smallest-range chart for timing entry and exit.

Guerilla: 5 second, 1 minute, 5 minutes.

Scalper: 1 minute, 5 minutes, 30 minutes.

Day trader: 5 minutes, 30 minutes, daily.

Position trader: 30 minutes, daily, weekly.

These are only general recommendations and may be adjusted to your own trading needs and propensities. Be sure you select a broker/dealer who offers the chart types and time frames you require for your trading.

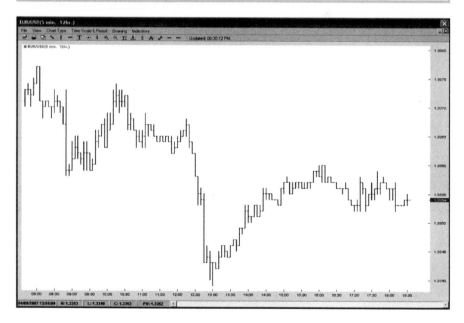

FIGURE 6.1 Trading Level Bar Chart Example 1.
Source: FXtrek IntelliChart™. Copyright 2001–2007 FXtrek.com, Inc.

FIGURE 6.2 Trading Level Bar Chart Example 2.
Source: FXtrek IntelliChart™. Copyright 2001–2007 FXtrek.com, Inc.

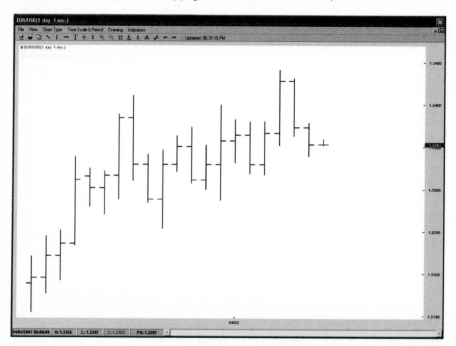

FIGURE 6.3 Trading Level Bar Chart Example 3.
Source: FXtrek IntelliChart™. Copyright 2001–2007 FXtrek.com, Inc.

Codex Markets

I recommend that all traders begin with a single market—the most popular one: USD/EUR. This pair represents the interaction between the two most widely held currencies in the world.

The first determination for selecting further markets to trade is your trader profile. The shorter term you decide to trade, the more volatile the markets you should seek.

Some factors are not quantifiable. If you like the looks of a market and how it trades, add it to your codex. Conversely, don't fight a market that treats you badly; deselect it and try another.

Currency Personalities

Some traders never figure out this simple and valuable fact: Different pairs and crosses exhibit their own personalities. These personalities do change, but typically only over a long period of time.

Personalities can be defined by the market environment factors of directional movement, volatility, thickness, and rhythm.

Over a period of time trading you will find currency personalities that agree with your style of trading—and personalities that do not. By keeping a record of basic ME characteristics in your codex notebook you will learn which are which.

I recommend a battery of five pairs and five crosses. As you trade, you will certainly find other markets that appeal to you. Be sure to have a good sense of their volatility before trading them. Watch a market for 30 days before ever trading in it. Get a fine-tuned sense of its personality.

Markets for Trader Profiles

My favorite FOREX markets. Work with Tier One, move on to Tier Two. Avoid Crosses and Exotics until you have mastered a few pairs.

The euro/U.S. dollar (EUR/USD) is the most popular pair traded. it offers lots of liquidity and variety for all trader profiles. Be aware of U.S. Federal Reserve announcements and U.S. Bureau of Labor and other governmental reports. These news items can have a powerful and immediate effect on prices, directional movement, and volatility. Pip spreads may balloon from 1 or 2 pips to 30 or more pips, especially if you are using a retail market-maker broker/dealer.

My advice: Stay out of the markets during these times. Sit on your hands and watch the reaction to the news for price trend indications. It is not uncommon for prices to react in one direction after news, only to gradually move back in the opposite direction over the course of the trading session.

Keep in mind that a market can look enormously different on different chart scales and also within different time frames. Use only your three bar charts and no others. A market's personality may look different on different bar charts, as a function of either the scale of the chart or the range of the chart. The same currency pair may exhibit different personalities and market environment characteristics over a 5-second chart, a 30-minute chart, and a daily chart. Don't let chart scales or ranges confuse you; it is easy to let this happen!

Chart Scales

Remember, how you configure a chart can make a world of difference. Try different colors and backgrounds. A 5-minute chart for 6 hours can look much different than a 5-minute chart for 24 hours. Trading platforms and chart services scale the data to fit the same size window. Select a time period that works for you and keep to it consistently. Even resizing a chart on your computer screen can make it appear different.

In FOREX little things mean a lot—it doesn't take much to throw a trader off stride!

Style and Market Environment

After you've decided on markets to trade, keep an informal record of their market environment characteristics. You'll soon find you do better with some ME combinations than with others. Armed with this information, you can more easily sort future potential selections and market candidates. Eyeballing a market involves watching the four market environment factors and the matrix of your three time-scale bar charts. With this simple and visual tool set, you will always be in very close touch with any market.

Psychology and Attitude

The sum total of all buy and sell orders determines what the market does and where it goes. But all traders are human, and the primary emotions of fear and greed lie hidden—sometimes not very deeply—beneath the buy and sell orders.

Even in this day of robots, black boxes, and computer-based trading with no human involvement in the order-entry process, fear and greed reign supreme. A human had to write the program, and that person's propensities for profit (greed) and loss (fear) are built into the code.

Your attitude and emotions will play some part in every aspect of your trading. Every decision you make, large or small, has an emotional component—from the tools you select to the markets you monitor, to when you enter and exit a market. They are always there, and denying them is a poor solution.

Controlling your emotions is the key to success. Knowing they are there, constantly monitoring them, and being able to keep them in check are your goals from the time you sit down to trade to the time you walk away from your computer.

Steps to Emotional Success

"Know thyself" is the old Socratic adage. Nowhere is it more important than in the markets. The more leveraged the markets, the faster and harder personality weaknesses will be driven to the surface.

Step One: I, Trader What sort of personality are you? We tend to define traits in terms of pairs or dichotomies: positive/negative, introverted/extroverted, calm/excitable. It is certainly possible any combinations from each dichotomy could define a successful trader. But the odds, and my experience over 30 years, seem to favor certain combinations over others.

A happy/extroverted/calm personality is probably the ideal successful trader candidate. I am a positive/introverted/calm type. The greatest trader I ever knew was Charles B. Goodman. He was a negative/introverted/calm personality.

Perhaps the most critical personality spectrum is calm/excitable. The markets want you to get excited. The excited person will tend to wear rose-colored or gray-colored glasses when making decisions. Human nature being what it is, we all tend to get excited at the most critical times—just when, as traders, we need to be calm.

The only way to avoid this dilemma is to know in advance that getting excited can and will happen. By monitoring your emotions, you can detect early clues of the onset of overexcitement. Part of this solution is the daily trade plan that I discuss in Part Four.

Keep notes of when emotions interfered with your trading—what markets, what time of day, at entry or exit, and so on. You'll soon see patterns, and just knowing what causes your emotions to come unglued is a big step in controlling them.

Step Two: Charting Your Emotions Use a chart to monitor your emotions. I have used biofeedback techniques and they have worked well for me. Other techniques are also effective.

Keep an hourly chart of your emotions for the spectrum that may give you the most problems as a trader or just on a per-session basis. If it is calm/excitable, as it is for most of us, make copies of a simple chart as shown in Figure 6.4. You are attempting to quantify an emotional quality and that is very difficult, but as a trader, you need something to help you consider your emotional state. It also provides a long-term record for review.

At the end of each week you may want to line up the markets you've been watching against your emotional points and observe for any correlations. You will be surprised at what you see and what you can learn. Perspective is sometimes enormously valuable to the trader.

Step Three: Handling Profits and Losses   The biggest driver of emotions is profit and loss. This is why paper trading is almost never particularly useful, at least with respect to seeing how good a trader you are in the long run. Profits make us happy and excited; losses make us sad and irritable.

Every new trader I have ever known has made money when trading a demo account. When they begin trading real money in a real account, things happen. The dynamics of trading real money are enormously different from trading for fun.

If profits and losses cause too big an emotional swing, you may be making trades involving too much money. There is an old saying, "Trade down to a good sleep." The money in play may be too much, or you are counting too heavily on success. Don't ever trade with money you couldn't afford to lose or give away to charity.

Don't count your chickens before they hatch. I have seen traders do so well on small accounts that they have quit their day jobs to trade full time, and they quickly fail. Trade as a hobby. If you ever get to the point where you have made a year or two years' income in the markets over some significant period of time, only then consider full-time, professional trading.

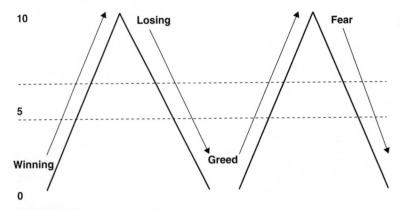

FIGURE 6.4 Emotional State Chart.

How much should you commit to trading? The simple answer is never trade with money you couldn't afford to lose or give away. That may be $500 or $500,000. If you make some substantial initial profits, *don't* get the King Kong syndrome, quit your day job, buy a $10,000 trading station, and order brochures from the local Mercedes dealer. *Do* add money to your account. Yes, add money. This is an old psychological trick Charlie taught me, and—for newbies with small accounts—it really works if only because it keeps the King Kong syndrome at bay.

How much should you commit to any specific trade? Many traders like to rate their trades, perhaps from 1 being a good trade to 3 being a fantastic opportunity. This may work when you have traded for a year or longer, but I don't recommend it initially; it's just one more parameter to juggle, one more decision to make. As a new trader, your pretrade ratings may not be accurate.

The "Trading Campaigns" table (see box) shows my recommendations for trade size vis-à-vis total account size. I offer more on this subject in Chapter 7. I recommend dividing your capital into 30 trading units with 10 units, or trades, in three different campaigns. I learned this from Bruce Gould, commodities trader extraordinaire, and it's golden. Mr. Gould is perhaps the sharpest money management guru in the trading business. His old newsletters from the 1970s and 1980s are available from his web site, www.brucegould.com, and are definitely worth reading by any new trader in stocks, commodities, or FOREX.

Trading Campaigns

$500	5,000 units
$2,500	10,000 units
$5,000	20,000 units
$10,000	50,000 units
$25,000	100,000 units

Each trader should adjust his three 10-trade campaigns according to the appropriate risk/reward and stop/profit level for his own trading profile.

As an alternative, you may trade by leverage ratio. Many broker/dealers allow you to trade fixed leverage ratios between 10:1 and 50:1. Start low (10:1) and go up gradually (15:1, 20:1) with each successful campaign.

Don't let losses discourage you. Even the best traders have periods of long losing streaks. My record is 16 lemons in a row. I came close to throwing in the towel. If you have several losses or a single large loss, the first thing to do is turn off your computer (after closing all your trades, of course) and take a break.

Make the break time long enough to accomplish two things: (1) Clear your head of trading and the intense emotion of the loss. This usually takes more than a few days. (2) When you feel refreshed and clearheaded, analyze the losses. What caused them and what can you do to prevent them from recurring? Make the appropriate adjustments and begin afresh, slowly. Don't dwell on losses or profits; come to each trading session fresh.

Another tip: Don't discuss your trading with anyone, at least not in any detail. Avoid trading clubs and getting addicted to the numerous FOREX blogs and forums now populating the Internet.

Ten Most Common Causes of Losing Trades

1. Overtrading.

2. Stops too close or unrealistic with respect to price objectives.

3. Spur-of-the-moment trading.

4. Trading high-volatility, high-directional-movement markets.

5. Trading the news instead of the reaction to it.

6. Trading outside of your market environment profile.

7. Trading crosses and exotics.

8. Trading over multiple sessions.

9. Trading when under duress.

10. Trading with money you cannot afford to lose.

Record Keeping

Accurate, honest record keeping is essential to knowing your emotions and keeping them at bay. By studying your trading records, you'll get all the feedback you need to see how emotions are affecting your trading. In Part Four I describe a daily and weekly trade plan and other records you should maintain.

If you can't keep a daily report, at least keep a diary at the end of each trading session. Whether you keep a diary or a report, each one should have attached a session chart of each market you traded. In this way, you can periodically review what you wrote vis-à-vis the markets you were trading at the time.

Summary

I wish I could be more objective and quantitative about psychology and attitude. But the nature of emotions is that they are qualitative and vary enormously

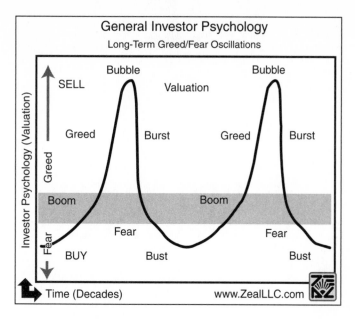

FIGURE 6.5 Don't Ride These Trends!

among traders. Each trader is unique and needs to think over all the factors involved and make his own *realistic* decisions. In trading, the Socratic admonition to "know thyself" is so very important.

If you have psychological or emotional weaknesses, nothing will bring them out faster, in the form of financial loss, than the markets. The more leveraged the market, the faster it will happen. (See Figure 6.5.) Consistently monitor your emotional state, keep good records, and frequently review your trades vis-à-vis your emotions. When you make mistakes, learn what you can from them and move on to the next trade with a clear head.

Making Money Management Decisions

The goal of money management is to break even.
                                        —Charles B. Goodman

Money management is neither sexy nor easy to come to grips with for most of us.

Because money management crosses over between trading tools and style, it is always somewhat subjective. It is almost a *soft* element, but it is possible to build a *hard* money-management framework. The trading campaign framework I discussed in the previous chapter is such an idea. As long as the trader doesn't stray from the framework, ad hoc and subjective decisions are possible without causing too much trouble. The markets are enormously dynamic and change is necessary. The key is to keep changes evolutionary instead of revolutionary.

Money Management Parameters

As I wrote in *Getting Started in Currency Trading*, there are three basic money management parameters to be considered. Although they are important individually, it is critical that they work together and aren't contradictory with each other or with your trader profile.

1. Trading capital.
2. Trade size.
3. Risk/reward (stop/profit objective).

These should all work in harmony with your trading profile. For example:

- Don't position-trade if your trading capital is $500.
- Don't trade 100,000 lots with $1,000 trading capital.
- If you are a scalper, don't expect to set 5-pip stops and 50-pip objectives.

Matching Profiles with Parameters

Now consider these three parameters in conjunction with your profile.

Guerillas: 10 · 3 trades per campaign, 15-pip objectives, and 10-pip stops.
Scalpers: 10 · 3 trades per campaign, 25-pip objectives, and 15-pip stops.
Day traders: 10 · 3 trades per campaign, 50-pip objectives, and 20-pip stops.
Position traders: 10 · 3 campaigns, 1-pip objectives, and 25-pip stops.

The longer term your trader profile allows, the lower can be your overall win-to-loss ratio.

Feel free to alter these parameters, at least slightly. But don't go *off-board*—that is, outside of them—too often without good reason.

Unrealistic Expectations

The guerilla profile on small trade capital is not recommended. Retail pip spreads, an occasional reversal, ballooning pip spreads on news, and inability to execute instantly are all reasons leading to failure.

The position profile on small capital is not recommended. The risk for the small trader staying over sessions is very high.

You can't have it all: Don't expect to both hit a high percentage of winning trades (50 percent or more) and also use very close stops (10 pips) and/or high-ratio risk/reward parameters (5:1 or more).

As you adopt new market pairs and crosses to trade, you will find with experience that some markets do require money management parameter adjustments. However, if a pair takes you out of your trading profile, perhaps it is better to seek another opportunity.

I talk about using this information in Parts 3 and 4. For now, we are happy to just add the basics to your codex.

Breaking Even

It may sound strange to hear that your overall goal is to break even. However, especially for the new trader, that is exactly how it should be. We know most new traders lose quickly and are shown the door long before they even have the time to develop their trading style or learn to use their trading tools. The best way to avoid this calamity—and be around to learn the markets and profit thereby—is to think about *risk* first, *reward* second.

Breaking even does not mean closing a trade after only a few minutes, although I have done that exact thing many times when I felt something was wrong or the market environment changed rapidly. As long as you don't overtrade, the costs of doing business in FOREX are small enough that the trader can afford such luxuries. If you start with the USD/EUR pair, you will pay only two or three pips per trade.

Statistically, you have a higher overall winning expectation with ten 10-pip loss trades than a single 100-pip loss. A 100-pip trade is a calamity to most traders; 10 pips is very survivable.

Breaking even does require giving most of your pretrade consideration to the risk involved in a trade. If a trade doesn't fit into your profile parameters, you had better make sure you have very substantial reasons for going off-board.

Trade Size

In Chapter 6, I discussed briefly setting a trade size and sticking with it. Each time you double your money—should you be so fortunate—you may then double your trade size.

If you're on a beer budget of $2,000 or less, you'll need to begin trading with what is called a mini-account. Most broker/dealers now offer mini-accounts. OANDA (www.oanda.com) and www.efxgroup.com are two you might consider; there are many more. You can work backward from your trader profile and money management parameters to determine a reasonable trade size based on the 10 · 3 trading campaign concept I introduced in Chapter 6.

Again, I recommend that newbies use a fixed-loss amount for each trade. The trade size calculation is:

$$\text{Risk per trade} = \frac{\text{Trading capital / 3 campaigns}}{10 \text{ trades}}$$

All other money management parameters can be derived from this formula and your trading profile.

Market Entry and Exit

The methods for market entry are numerous. Some traders use charts to enter and exit a trade, some traders use ad hoc rule sets, and others use indicators.

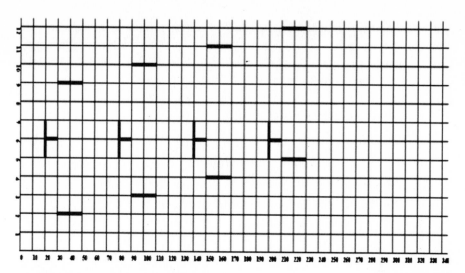

FIGURE 7.1 Fixed Price Stops.
Beginner traders should start trading with fixed price stops and fixed price profit objectives. Each successively higher trading profile may realistically set higher and higher risk/reward ratios.

Entry and exit off a chart is the most transparent; you don't have to translate the meaning of one tool to another to make a decision. It is also faster, and the markets move so quickly that whoever hesitates is indeed lost.

Exit is a little different from entry. You make an independent decision to enter a market. Exit decisions may be due to your profit target being attained and/or the market hitting your stop-loss. Those new to FOREX should set a stop-loss order for their fixed loss amount as soon as they have confirmation of a market entry. See Figure 7.1.

My FxCodex approach uses the entry and exit techniques inherent in *Getting Started in Currency Trading,* namely GSCS. I show you more of these in Part Three. In Chapter 8, I discuss using GSCS to both enter and exit the market. For now, use it only to enter, and add the exit techniques later, after you have had a few months' experience trading.

I believe any codex approach should use the chart entry and exit method, if not with GSCS, then with some other internalized technique, even if it is a fixed price method.

Monitoring a Trade

Between entry and exit, there is not too much the trader can or should do beyond keeping the trade closely under observation. You've made your decisions, paid your money—now it's time to watch. Use this time to examine other candidate trades or update your reports. Don't use it to troll the blogs or forums.

There are reasons you may be advised to close an active position before it either attains your profit objective or hits your stop-loss:

Reasons to Close an Active Trade

- An unexpected announcement is pending.
- The market environment changes suddenly.
- You are called away for a period of time from the markets.
- Your Internet or trading platform goes down.
- You suffer an emotional crisis.

Processes work best the less they are interrupted or altered. If you find yourself frequently closing an active trade, it may be time to reexamine the process itself.

Summary

From the information in this chapter, you should determine your trader profile and complementary money market parameters, including trade size and stop-loss values. Add all this information to your codex notebook along with the trading techniques you have selected for your personal codex.

Setting Up Your Trading Platform

You'll make most of your money sitting on your hands.

—Charles B. Goodman

I n the codex approach to FOREX trading, all the elements must work together in harmony. This includes the broker/dealer trading platform, sometimes referred to as a trading station.

Selecting a Broker/Dealer

Selecting a broker/dealer is discussed in detail in *Getting Started in Currency Trading (GSICT)*. Since that book was written, we can all be grateful for a number of happy occurrences. Many of the borderline broker/dealers are gone. New capital requirement rules have taken effect, and all the major trading platforms have become both more stable and more robust. In fact, so many features exist in a typical dealing station that it sometimes becomes confusing.

Most of the major broker/dealers also have arrangements with third-party vendors, which allows you a great deal of flexibility in selecting a toolbox. However, I recommend starting with just the charting tools integrated into your broker/dealer's trading platform.

Your primary interest is in broker/dealers' bar charts, because these are the backbone of the codex trading approach.

The first criteria (beyond the due diligence covered in Chapter 5 of *GSICT*) are the look and feel. How do the charts look to you? What about the overall feel of the platform? This is strictly a personal choice. Select a market pair and a specific time range and time frame. Look at and work with this chart from several broker/dealers. Remember that most trade stations allow you to customize the look and feel of a chart.

You'll be watching the screen for many hours, so make a good initial choice and try to stick with it. Just changing chart color schemes midcourse can be an enormous distraction. Spend some time here and try to stick with your selections. Figures 8.1 and 8.2 will give you an idea how different parameters can make charts look much different.

Demo Account

If you are a new FOREX trader, you should download the demo of at least four or five broker/dealers and spend a few hours working with each of them.

The second criterion is the feature set. Does the trading platform have the tool set you need and the money management capabilities? Appendix B

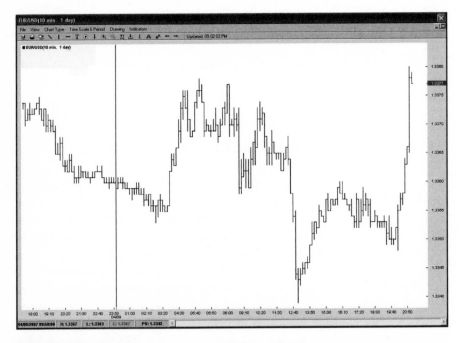

FIGURE 8.1   Sample Chart 1: A 10-Minute, 1-Day Chart.
Colors, chart size, and time frame can all create a different look and feel.
Experiment with a variety of trading stations and find the ones that seem best to you. Then stick with them.
Source: FXtrek IntelliChart™. Copyright 2001–2007 FXtrek.com, Inc.

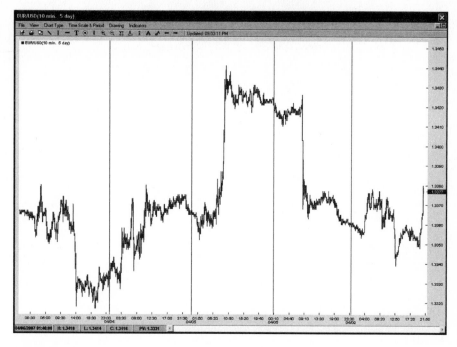

FIGURE 8.2 Sample Chart 2: A 10-Minute, 5-Day Chart.
Shading, color (if you use other than black and white) and sizes can alter
the appearance of a chart dramatically.
Source: FXtrek IntelliChart™. Copyright 2001–2007 FXtrek.com, Inc.

contains a list of broker/dealers meeting codex requirements with respect to
feature set. None of them have everything, however. As I have mentioned,
swing charts are not popular right now and are more difficult to find.

All retail broker/dealers offer a demo account. (See Figure 8.3.) Try at
least five of them, more if possible.

Be sure a trading platform has as many as possible of the tools you need
and use. You can find almost anything from third-party vendors, but the more
your primary platform includes, the better and easier it is for the trader. Just a
few of the more popular:

www.efxgroup.com

www.oanda.com

www.gftFOREX.com

www.hotspotfx.com

www.gaincapital.com

Most brokers ask for only the basic information to open a demo account.

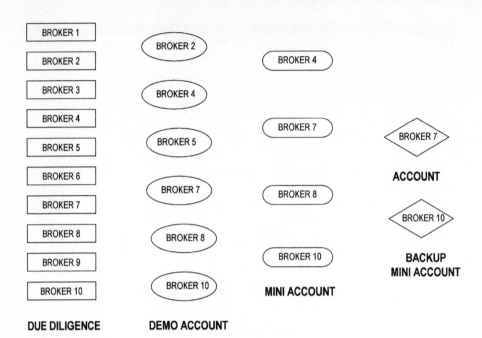

FIGURE 8.3 The Account Due Diligence Process.

Be sure a trading platform has as many as possible of the tools you need and use. You can find almost anything from third-party vendors, but the more your primary platform includes, the better and easier it is for the trader. Just a few of the more popular:

> www.gaincapital.com
> www.efxgroup.com
> www.FOREX.com
> www.gftFOREX.com
> www.hotspotfx.com

Most brokers ask for only the most basic information for a Demo account but you will be on their mailing list.

Setting Up Your Trading Platform

The two most critical features you will need to trade the codex approach are bar charts and flexible stop capabilities. If you can *trade from the chart*, that will be a small but significant advantage. Some of the newer dealer platforms allow you to simply click on the chart to execute a trade, rather than manually enter a price.

One feature I miss is being able to set the range values on charts; these are automatically set for the trader when the trader selects the time scale.

If and when you trade multiple markets, you will probably want a computer system with two separate monitors. You can, of course, keep multiple browser sessions open, but clicking from one to another can be distracting. One of the monitors will be for your actual trading activities, the other(s) for your charts.

For trading the codex method, you need three bar charts for each pair or cross you are trading. How you organize charts is up to you. Experiment as much as you like, but be fully satisfied with the arrangement before trading.

After you've selected a broker/dealer and a trading platform, it is time to set it up for trading. Having spent some time with the broker/dealer's demo account, you should be comfortable with the methods for doing a simple setup. The key elements are your charts. You'll want full visual reference to your three bar charts according to your trader profile for the USD/EUR. If you have space, add the primary (middle chart time frame) of three other pairs (not crosses) that appear to meet your personal codex criteria.

The author had hoped to show the reader a typical trading platform setup. We asked permission from five different broker-dealers: Gain Capital, EFXgroup, DukasCopy, FXsol, and HotSpotFX. Gain Capital was kind enough to reply and was anxious to oblige, but because of third-party charts was unable to oblige. The others did not respond to our request.

I recommend the serious FOREX trader have at least a 20-inch widescreen monitor with a high-end graphics card. Many traders use multiple monitors; I've seen systems with a dozen monitors. I use two monitors—one for my dealing station and one for my charts. You can manage everything on one monitor but the constant opening, closing, and resizing of windows can be distracting and time-consuming.

Initially you will find following three charts for a single pair to be a full time job. As you gain experience you will become more comfortable watching multiple markets. Everyone has a limit, in psychology it is called 'channel capacity' and your trading method also impacts how many markets you can track comfortably. My limit seems to be five or six and I am very comfortable with three or four.

Overkill

The key to success is spending most of your trading time analyzing a few markets very thoroughly and minimizing distractions that force you to change focus too often. Keep it simple.

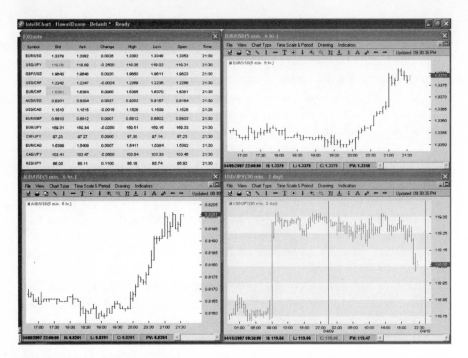

FIGURE 8.4 Charting Services.

FXtrek (www.FXtrek.com), maker of IntelliCharts, has a superior charting service. It is integrated or can be integrated into some broker/dealer trading platforms.

Source: FXtrek IntelliChart™. Copyright 2001–2007 FXtrek.com, Inc.

I have seen trade stations for individual traders with up to fifteen monitors! That is overkill. I simply don't think an inexperienced trader can follow so many markets, charts and indicators—and make a rational decision about a trade. Frequently shifting from one market to another is not good. Two monitors should do; one for your broker-dealer platform, another for charts and indicators. You may wish to keep your primary markets on the monitor with your trading platform. Use the second monitor to host charts of your secondary and tertiary markets. If you do need ultra-high power and multiple monitors, check out: www.alienware.com and www.tradingcomputers.com. Do not forget a backup power supply and a backup internet connection.

Tip—do not skimp on either the quality of your monitor(s) or graphics card. When you get rich from trading and retire to Hawaii you will want to save your eyesight for the sunsets.

Summary

This concludes Part Two of *Getting Started in FOREX Trading Strategies*. You have now assembled a toolbox, defined at least your initial trading style, and decided your money management parameters. You've selected and explored a broker/dealer's trading station with a demo account and perhaps worked with some of the choices residing in your codex. Finally, you've done the initial setup on your trade station with charts, stop-loss parameters, and any of the other codex tools the platform offers.

You do know the trading platform inside and out and are extremely comfortable with using it. You *don't* know how to put all of this together as yet, but you are already ahead of 90 percent of all traders with respect to trade preparation.

Part

The Codex Method of Trading FOREX

Chapter 9

Tracking Markets

Fear and greed loom large once you take a position in the market.
—Charles B. Goodman

We are now ready to walk through a trade and show how the various elements—toolbox, style, and money management—work within the codex process. I include information on tactics and market filters in this chapter because they are easier to understand with specific examples.

Part Three is very visual. I've used many screenshots from the Gain Capital www.gaincapital.com trading platform to show the codex process in action. Whatever broker/dealer and trading platform you select, the similarities will be much greater than any differences.

There are six steps in the codex trade process: (1) tracking, (2) analyzing and selecting, (3) entering, (4) monitoring, (5) exiting, and (6) reviewing.

The Process in Review

Tracking → Selecting → Entry → Monitoring → Exit → Postmortem

---

It may help to look at the process in reverse. Our goal is to complete a winning trade in the USD/EUR pair market.

We will use GSCS as our primary tool to make our entry and exit from the market. I am using only two of the GSCS ideas in this part of the book: the double intersection and the return. I also emphasize ordinal rules over cardinal rules.

If you decide to use GSCS as your primary chart interpretation method, use only the ordinal principles first; there are many good trades waiting to be made this way. After you have mastered the ordinal rules and feel confident in your ability and experiences, you can concentrate on the cardinal rules.

My web site, www.fxpraxis.com, has a Goodman Discussion Board for those who trade with me through my Introducing Broker relationship. The GSCS section of the web site also has other Goodman articles, including a time-based counting system for advanced traders.

The codex approach uses bar charts, swing charts, or point and figure charts to monitor and define a market within the context of your trader profile.

Tracking Candidates

The first step is the act of finding qualified candidate trades. If you have no active trade in the market, then you are monitoring both the EUR/USD pair and the three monitor pairs you selected.

Primary, Secondary, and Tertiary Markets		
Tier 1: USD Major	*Tier 2: USD Major*	*Tier 3: Cross Rate*
EUR/USD	GBP/USD	EUR/GBP
USD/JPY	AUD/USD	AUD/JPY
GBP/USD	USD/CHF	GBP/CHF

New traders should focus only on tier 1 pairs and move on to tier 2 pairs and tier 3 crosses only after success in tier 1.

After you have traded for a few weeks, the three-tier approach is ideal. Initially, I recommend only two tiers:

- Tier 1: the three charts of the USD/EUR selected in accordance with your profile.
- Tier 2: the three candidate markets for which you are monitoring only the middle-range chart. For candidates, I recommend pairs that show a relatively high degree of thickness. Don't trade or monitor crosses (pairs not including the USD) until you have traded with real money in your account for several months.

Two Market Tiers

Tier 1 Chart Scales

Guerilla trader: tick, 1 minute, 5 minute.

Scalper: 1 minute, 5 minute, 15 minute.

Day trader: 5 minute, 30 minute, 1 hour.

Position trader: 30 minute, 1 hour, daily.

Tier 2 Chart Scales

Guerilla trader: 1 minute.

Scalper: 5 minute.

Day trader: 30 minute.

Position trader: 1 hour.

All traders should step back and review the price behavior on daily and weekly charts at least once a week.

I use bar charts exclusively to monitor candidate markets. GSCS is used to select trades and enter and exit the market. The other tools in the FxCodex toolbox I use primarily to check my conclusions and perhaps catch opportunities I may have missed.

Look at your candidates from several perspectives:

- Does the market under consideration meet your stylistic requirements? Directional movement, volatility, thickness, and rhythm should all be examined.
- How do those characteristics match up with your profile? See Table 9.1.

Candidate Markets

Candidates should meet all of these criteria:

- Appropriate pair or cross.
- Suitable market environment.
- Good money management.
- GSCS criteria.

TABLE 9.1 Candidate Markets versus Profile		
Profile	Yes	No
Pair (cross)		
Market environment		
Money management		
GSCS criteria		

If the candidates' characteristics match up well with your profile, continue. If they don't, keep monitoring. Never accept a less-than-perfect-looking
candidate. Sit on your hands until one shows itself to you.

Does the candidate have the basic swing characteristics for a GSCS trade?
You will need some experience with GSCS—or whatever interpretive method
your codex includes—to make this determination intelligently. If you are using
GSCS, stick with the return and double intersection formations for now. This
requires anticipating how formations are built over time and requires a bit of
experience. The more charts you study, the more you will be able to quickly
spot candidates. See Figures 9.1 and 9.2.

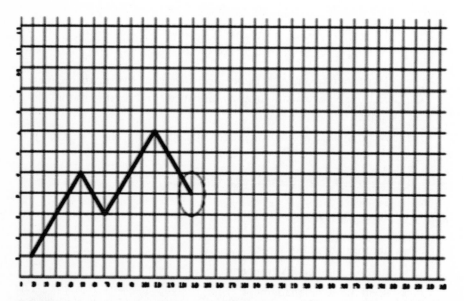

FIGURE 9.1 A Goodman Return Candidate.
This is the basic paradigm for a return candidate. The fourth wave
(endpoint circled) is the critical return wave.

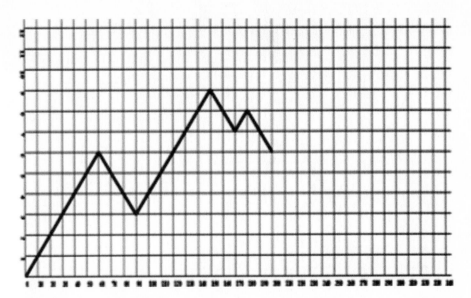

FIGURE 9.2 A Goodman Double Intersection Candidate.
This is the basic paradigm for a double intersection candidate. The circled
endpoint represents the double intersection of the 50 percent move of two
waves—the waves of the first three smaller waves and the wave of the third
wave. It is the author's considered opinion, after 30 years in the market,
that the return and double intersection are the two most useful formations
in all of trading. For more information please see "Currency Codex" on
www.fxpraxis.com.

Look for markets with the appropriate characteristics and attempt to visualize the GSCS wave potentials in them. See Figure 9.3.

Summary

For a potential trade to move from *candidate* to *select*, it must meet further criteria; to move from *select* to *trade*, even more. This layered process approach
can seem tedious and at times boring. Most trades will never make it all the
way from *candidate* to *trade* status.

When you are able to watch two or three markets and monitor four or
five more, you will have all the opportunities you can handle, irrespective of
your profile.

Because you are actively trading only a single market (USD/EUR), the
time between trades may be longer than you would like. The guerilla and the
scalper will find more trades than the day or position trader simply by virtue of
the time frames of the charts selected by each type of trader.

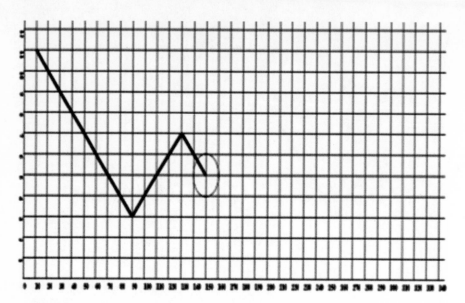

FIGURE 9.3 Waves in Progress—Mapping.
Anticipating wave propagation is key to success in trading GSCS. Which
wave is primary and which wave is secondary? In this example, is wave
3 the beginning of wave 3 of the first wave or is it wave 2 of the second
wave? Reference to the next larger chart scale often provides important
clues. If this is a 15-minute chart, refer to the hourly chart to determine the
primary trend of the market.

But by using this filtering process, you are assured not to miss anything in
your codex. The trades you make will be the strongest of the strong.

Selecting Markets

Passing a good trade is better than making a bad one.
—Charles B. Goodman

A selected candidate is a strong candidate, but it is not a trade just yet. It needs to meet more criteria to move up the ladder.

Perspective

Everyone wants to trade the major trend of the market. But what is the major trend? To a guerilla it may be the direction on a five-minute chart, while a position trader may reference something as broad as a weekly chart for perspective.

I am using a day trade as an example, and assume you are keeping in mind the codex adjustments required to make it pertinent to you. For my work, the perspective chart is a daily chart. I want to trade the daily trend, or at least the session trend.

Perhaps your losing trades occur mostly when you fight the perspective chart trend? Chapter 14 discusses post-trade diagnostics.

Close Examination

Next, go the other direction and examine the elements of the trade, beginning with your detail chart. Does anything there contradict your selection? If you are using GSCS, what are the smaller formations telling you? Do they confirm the trade chart?

Not all markets are good Goodman candidates. But given three pairs trades and three chart scales you will find enough opportunities that you can be selective. Markets with high volatility and low directional movement should be passed up.

GSCS Characteristics

Directional movement: medium to high.
Volatility: low to medium.
Rhythm: regular.
Thickness: medium to high.

Confirming Evidence

Here I would look for any confirming Nofri formations and make sure the TMA and TOA indicators are also confirming. If you are using any indicators, now is the time to look at them and see what they are telling you about the market.

This is the perfect time to eyeball the chart. Look for the four eyeball characteristics:

- Directional movement
- Volatility
- Rhythm
- Thickness

Nofri Characteristics

Nofri trades rely more on rhythm than the other market environment characteristics. Rhythm should be regular.

Directional movement: low to high.
Volatility: low to high.
Rhythm: regular.
Thickness: low to high.

Money Management Parameters

Where will your initial stop belong? Where is your objective? Does the ratio of the two fit into your money management parameters? If not, it's a pass until or unless they come into conformance.

Tactics and Filters

Look at your trading calendar for the two currencies making the pair. Are any announcements pending? Has an announcement been made recently and is the market still working it off?

What time of day is it? Check charts going back a week or two for the same time period. Does the market exhibit erratic behavior this time of day, or does it generally behave normally? By *erratic*, I mean exhibiting volatility spikes or sharp changes in directional movement. See Figure 10.1.

Back to our old friends of directional movement—volatility and thickness. Have any of these changed dramatically on the trade chart recently?

What are the eyeballing characteristics—directional movement, volatility, thickness, and rhythm? Are they steady? Have they changed recently?

Mapping the Trade

If you are using GSCS now, try to visualize your ideal outcome. Then visualize alternative outcomes and—especially—the worst-case scenario. See Figure 10.2.

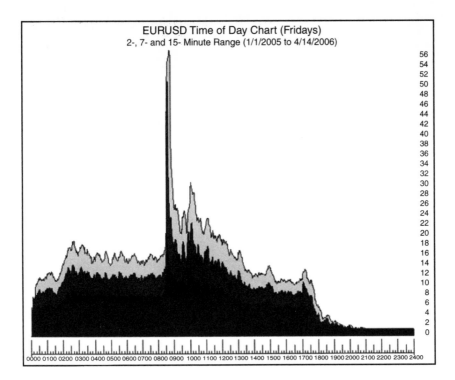

FIGURE 10.1 Time of Day.
Avoid the peak volatility periods. This coincides with Federal Reserve and other USD announcements. Caution: Pip spreads for some broker/dealers may expand enormously during these periods, up to 30 pips for the EUR/USD—another good reason to sit on your hands.

FIGURE 10.2 Visualize the Possibilities.
This chart of the AUD/USD has excellent GSCS and Nofri characteristics. The AUD/USD is typically a good trader for beginners with a reliable mid-range market environment profile.
Source: FXtrek IntelliChart™. Copyright 2001–2007 FXtrek.com, Inc.

Close Your Eyes

Finally, close your eyes for a full minute (unless you are a guerilla trader; then keep it to 10 seconds!). Think of something pleasant other than the markets. Clear your head and ask yourself whether your emotions have been making the decisions or your codex.

Summary

If everything is in alignment, your candidate is on high priority. It's time to pull the trigger and make a trade.

Making a Trade

Only pull the trigger if the gun is loaded.

—Charles B. Goodman

The actual trade process is relatively short and simple. All the decisions have been made and all the criteria of your codex have been examined. What remains is to look for an entry point and place an initial stop-loss order.

How Did We Get Here?

Let us review the codex process thus far. There are almost as many methods for timing market entry as there are trading tools.

Entry Techniques
- Volatility
- System
- Ratio
- Support/resistance

Similar to placing stops, an entry may be based on volatility, your trading system, or on a flat ratio where profit objective and stop are calculated a priori as a function of your trading profile.

I do not recommend either entry or stops based on support and resistance levels. These are used by so many traders that they seem to occur too often at the same price. Professional traders and unscrupulous broker/dealers look to run through these areas, then take a position in the opposite direction.

The FXCodex Entry Technique

After I have a fully selected candidate to trade, I use one of two entry methods. The *dagger* method is the simplest, but you may not always get the opportunity to use it because it requires the market to meet certain conditions. The *breakaway* method can be used if the dagger isn't a possibility.

You may use the same methods to exit a trade, assuming you have not been stopped out or your price objective reached. See Figures 11.1 and 11.2.

Use the mapping possibilities you've visualized to help determine entry.

The Initial Stop-Loss

What is true for entry also goes for stops. There are a variety of methods. See Figure 11.3.

Stops are often a mirror image of entry, although the trader has less flexibility because he already has a commitment to the market. Again, the stop-loss can be based on one these factors:

Volatility

System

Ratio

Support/resistance

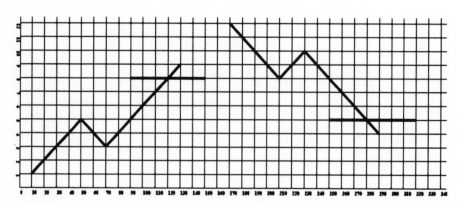

FIGURE 11.1 The Breakaway Entry Method.
Once you are certain you wish to enter a market, look for a small breakaway movement on the smallest chart scale you are using. Entries and exits should always be found on the smallest chart scale for your trader profile. The horizontal line represents where the wave has broken out by exceeding the measured move for that wave. This method requires specific price measurements to occur; thus it is called a cardinal technique.

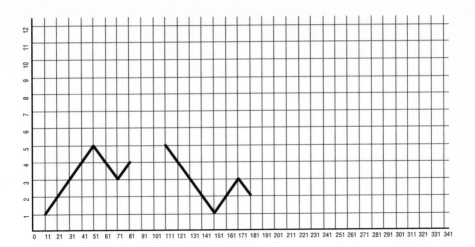

FIGURE 11.2   The Dagger Entry Method.
(1) Wait for the major trend to be defined. (2) Wait for a reaction to the
major trend. (3) Enter on the first significant price movement back in the
direction of the major trend. Close stops may be placed below the
beginning point of the secondary reaction wave. This method does not
rely on specific price measurements and is an ordinal technique.

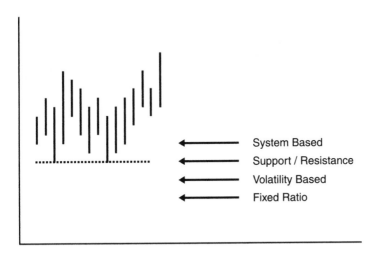

FIGURE 11.3   Stop Loss Techniques.

For a *volatility* stop simply calculate the average volatility of the market over
20 or 30 time units and place the stop slightly more than that distance from the
lowest price bar. A *system* stop is determined by one's trading system. A *ratio* stop
is determined by your profit objective and trader profile. A day trader might have
an objective of 100 pips and place a ratio stop at 25 pips. *Support* and *resistance*
stops are placed below support or above resistance. I do not recommend them.

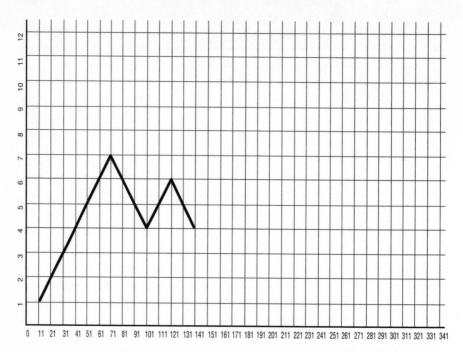

FIGURE 11.4 Stops and Waves.
Place a stop at a point where the GSCS wave is not forming according to your prediction. In this example, you expected wave 3 to carry past the high point of wave 1. It has also exceeded the 50 percent return of wave 3, giving indications that the primary wave may be wave 2 and not wave 1. GSCS stops will also help you avoid the support and resistance areas where many traders place their stops.

Ratio and volatility stops are the most manageable for the new trader. The FxCodex method places an initial stop at the point where the GSCS formation we are hoping to ride would be broken. For your first trades, I recommend a fixed value stop as described in Chapter 3.

The mapping possibilities can also help you locate an initial stop position. The point at which a wave is no longer behaving as predicted is a natural stop point. See Figure 11.4.

Summary

Something to keep in mind at this stage in the process is that when a trade is active, the only process action you can be actively involved with is monitoring the trade and waiting to see if your judgment proves to have been correct.

Monitoring a Trade

Watch your trades as you would watch your little children.
                                           —Charles B. Goodman

It is not difficult to monitor a trade. You've already done all the hard work of monitoring candidates, selecting and qualifying the candidate, and entering the trade.

The job of monitoring involves two duties:

1. Watching for unexpected news events or price action (they often go together) that might necessitate bailing out of the trade.

2. Moving your stop-loss as the trade works in your favor to first guarantee and then maximize the profit from the trade.

Use both your mapping possibilities and eyeballing for early indications that a trade may be going sour. Don't be afraid to exit a trade if it starts to become unpredictable or out of character. However, don't close out a trade just because you are nervous, if it still meets most of your criteria. It's a thin line between staying and leaving; only experience will help you develop the appropriate skills. Remember Charlie's old adage: "I made most of my money sitting on my hands!"

What If the Music Stops?

It often seems that as soon as we enter a market, it goes quiet. This happens because it is generally only active markets that attract our attention, and even active markets can go quiet for a time.

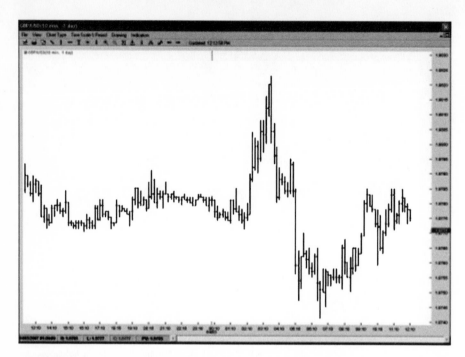

FIGURE 12.1   Quiet Markets.
This GBP/USD was a quiet trade that suddenly exploded. In FOREX, quiet markets seldom last for long periods of time!
Source: FXtrek IntelliChart™. Copyright 2001–2007 FXtrek.com, Inc.

It is true: You will make most of your money sitting on your hands—either monitoring a market, waiting patiently for your profit objective, or passing on markets that don't exactly meet your criteria. If you have to trade something in the absence of the perfect opportunity, trade quiet markets. See Figure 12.1.

Here is where you must sit on your hands and wait for the trade's outcome—the market's verdict.

Intersession or Fresh Start?

If you are either a guerilla or a scalper, you will never stay over a single session. Certainly, never stay over if you can't watch the markets full-time. It is better to close out your active trades and begin anew later.

Day traders will occasionally stay over between trading sessions—sometimes two, three, or more. It is impossible to stay awake that long, so stops in the market are required when you are away. Position traders may stay a week or longer, but in FOREX that is very, very rare.

The length of time you stay in the market can cut both ways. On the positive side, prices can move further over time and you can make more money with a trade. On the negative side, the longer you are in the market, the higher the probability is that a disconcerting news event will strike or the overall makeup of the market will shift dramatically. Volatility, directional movement, and/or thickness will morph. These factors may or may not impact your trade negatively or positively, but they all spell R-I-S-K.

For the new trader, I do not recommend keeping any active position in the market when you are not online and watching it full-time.

Monitoring Criteria

Watch for unusually swift changes in a market's makeup. Changes in volatility, directional movement, and/or thickness can indicate that something is afoot in that market. You don't necessarily have to bail out (or you may want to do so and just watch the action), but you should be prepared for unexpected price activity and have your stops well placed.

Trailing Stops

Trailing stops always sound like a great idea—until you trail the stop just a little too close, get stopped out, and leave a big part of your profitable trade on the table.

Be conservative in how far you trail stops away from the market and how often you move them. When you look at your trading activity over a year, you'll see that the outstanding trades are what carried you, and you can't get those by being prematurely stopped out of the market.

It sounds like a good idea to use trailing stops to protect your profit as it builds. But don't move your stops too often. Remember that each order you place in the market is a decision—and each decision has the potential of being a good one or being a bad one. The markets are a process, and the less you interfere with the process, the better off you will be in the long run. Use trailing stops gingerly, and raise or lower them according to all the criteria you used for selecting the initial stop, not just because you're bored and looking for something to do. Before moving a trailing stop up or down, wait for unusually high volatility and then move your stop just below or above that point. See Figure 12.2.

Don't let a decent profit get away. If the market is close to your objective and begins to vacillate, or if some of the four eyeballing characteristics change—*bail!*

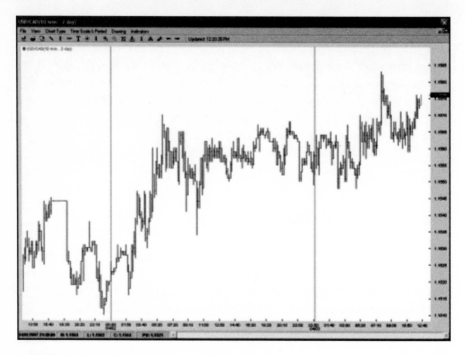

FIGURE 12.2 Trailing Stops—Good and Bad.
A trader long this USD/CAD market would need patience. Stops could be raised *after* the downward thrusts occur and the market begins to move back up.

Market environment characteristics—directional movement, volatility, thickness, and rhythm—usually change gradually, but not always. Be aware of the ME profile of the market you are trading and watch for ME changes as a clue to consider exiting soon. See Figure 12.3.

The greater the time scale unit of a chart, the more slowly market environment characteristics will change. On very long-term charts (daily, weekly) they seem extraordinarily consistent, partially because few traders are watching them or trading off them. Even to the guerilla trader, long-term charts offer valuable perspective.

Summary

The critical issue in monitoring a trade is to keep an objective attitude. You will feel a sense of ownership with an open position, and that isn't a particularly wise emotion. Try to stay objective and detached. Other than moving your stops, there is not a great deal you can do after a trade has been executed. Either you take your profit or your stop-loss gets elected.

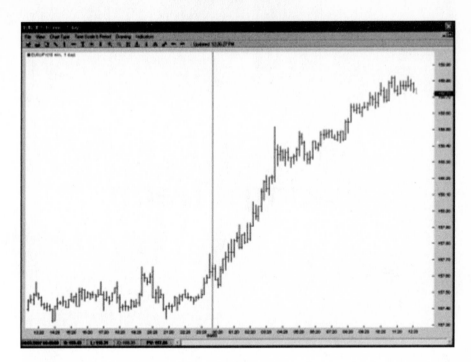

FIGURE 12.3 A Changing Market Environment.
In this example of the EUR/JPY, directional movement changed quickly although thickness stayed somewhat constant.

Exiting a Trade

Jacks or better open, but they rarely win the hand.
—Charles B. Goodman

I f you are superstitious, Chapter 13 may not be a happy choice for a chapter on exiting the market!

We want to exit from our profit objective, not from a stop-loss. This is a three-step process.

Steps to Exiting a Trade

First, set a rational profit objective, then monitor the profit objective to see if it changes. It should only change slightly, if at all, if you've done your work correctly. When your profit objective is met, exit the trade; don't let greed alter your decision. Let's look at the former possibility first.

Setting a Profit Objective

If you are using GSCS as your primary tool, set profit objectives according to your swing measurements. It is better to lower your profit objective than to make it too high. If the market runs, a trailing stop can be used to capture more profit than you expected. But never overstay your welcome!

Monitoring a Profit Objective

This is the time to sit on your hands. If you did your work, let the trade play out. Exit the trade from your profit objective or stop whenever possible. Watch for changes in the market environment and your wave failing to perform as expected.

The market neither knows nor cares if you are in or out, if you get stopped out or meet your profit objective. Don't anthropomorphize the market.

Meeting a Profit Objective

There is no better feeling than a trade completed with a profit. Don't second-guess your objective on any specific trade. But if your periodic trade review shows your objectives to be too high or too low, make minor—not major—adjustments to your process.

But sometimes you get stopped out of a trade. If you're a guerilla or scalper, it will happen very often, so you need to learn to deal with these events effectively and unemotionally.

No one enjoys being stopped out, but good traders learn to live with losses. If your stops are hit too regularly, you may be placing them too close. Are they realistic with respect to the volatility of a market? Does the stop point actually represent the failure of a wave? Analyze your losses regularly and objectively. (See Figure 13.1.) New traders should use fixed ratio stops initially. Move on to adjusting for volatility, and later, only after some experience trading, use system stops.

During the course of a trade there is often enormous pressure to either take profits ahead of an objective or move a stop-loss order. These sort of ad hoc decisions normally turn out badly, and they also violate the concept of trading as a process. Unless new information has entered the market that would have altered your earlier stop-loss or price objective, don't do it. News events can impact prices dramatically; let your profit objective and stop orders do their work for you; don't second-guess either the market or your own trading decisions.

Remember, this is only one trade; you intend to be in the market for a long time and make many, many trades. It is the after-trade postmortem where you should decide if your selection of price objectives or stop-loss was improper. Make your adjustments going forward, not going backward.

If you find you often have the temptation to alter price objectives or stops during a trade, you may wish to examine both your decision-making process and your emotional attachment to a trade. Watch the market for a short time after you exit. Don't draw conclusions on the basis of a single trade, but after 10 or more trades perhaps you can see a pattern such as placing stops too close or too far away. The trading process is continuous and doesn't start and stop with the beginning or end of each specific trade.

Keeping Tabs

Keep a record of all your trade statistics: number of winners and losers per every 10 trades, average winning trade dollar value, and average losing trade dollar value.

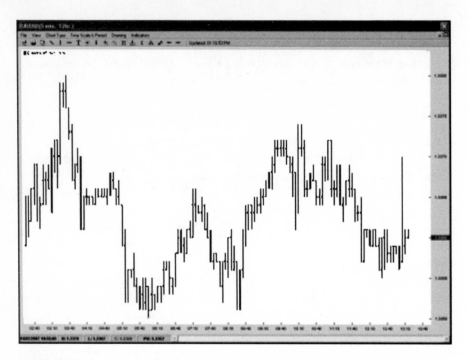

FIGURE 13.1 Stopped Out!
This EUR/USD had a near perfect 1-2-3 wave and return early. But the rapidly changing thickness and directional movement would have made stops difficult to place anytime later.

Summary

Traders tend to release their pent-up emotions when a trade is completed. If they made a profit, elation is natural. If they lost money by being stopped out, discouragement and even depression may well come to the surface.

Elation has a tendency to make us want to trade more and make more money, because after a winning trade it all seems so easy! Avoid the King Kong "I can do no wrong" syndrome.

Conversely, when we are discouraged, we tend to hang back, afraid. Both emotional responses are very natural, but the winning trader recognizes these tendencies and consciously works to pull his emotions back into a narrow band.

The markets neither like you nor hate you; they are not out to get you, either. Try not to develop the common habit of giving anthropomorphic tendencies to an inanimate process that has no interest in your activities, one way or the other.

Part 4

The Complete FOREX Trader

Postmortem and Record Keeping

After a trade, grieve or celebrate—then move on to the next opportunity.
—Charles B. Goodman

Why Keep Tracking Records?

You should do a postmortem of every completed trade and keep records and summaries of your trading activity, for several reasons. Perhaps the most important relates to the codex concept of *process*. All processes have feedback loops. If something goes wrong in the process—in this case, a losing trade—it is caught and analyzed in the feedback loop.

The famous ISO 9000 standard is an excellent example of a process with feedback evaluation. When something goes wrong, a corrective action ticket is written and the process is adjusted accordingly. Your notebook reports should include at least similar diagnostic information. Format is not critical but having a record of your conclusions is very useful. Over a number of trades, you will see patterns in your trading and analysis that improve your performance.

The constant feedback loop also prevents errors from welling up and necessitating a major overhaul of the process instead of simply an adjustment.

Feedback Loop

In the codex process each element talks to the other elements. For example, your trading tools must match both your trading style and money management approach.

Trading Tools fi Money Management fi Style

Another good reason to keep consistent records is to be able to take the pulse of your emotional state, thereby obligating yourself to stay with the process itself. Record keeping will assist you to not stray from the straight and narrow path of your codex.

Codex Records

Following are the reports you should be using, along with an explanation of how to organize and maintain them.

The Trade Log

This is the report you'll maintain on each trade, beginning with monitoring. Because many trades you begin monitoring won't become actual trades, some of the logs will be incomplete. But keep them anyway, as a way of reviewing your thinking and progress as well as your actual trades.

Alternatively, you may want to keep the trade log as a function of the steps in your codex. This method is a little less time consuming, but more difficult to keep track of over a long period of time.

Begin to devise a classification method for keeping track of your logs, whichever approach you decide to use. Define some consistent terms and symbols to use.

Elements of the Trade Log   Keep an accurate record of all your trades. Break them into (1) a single ledger, (2) weekly, and (3) monthly. If you use the trading campaign method outlined in Part One, also keep them grouped by each campaign. Most broker/dealer trading platforms allow you to customize the record of your trades but you will still want to at least export that information to your codex notebook.

Record at least the following information:

- Pair or cross traded.
- Entry and exit dates.

- Profit or loss in dollars.
- Profit or loss in pips.

The Trade Summary

For each trade completed, you will want to add a short summary. This doesn't need to be long or involved. One or two paragraphs summarizing the trade is enough. If the summary entails some research—a new idea, a corrective action—attach that to the summary when it is complete. Do your daily report the same day that the trade is closed, while it is still fresh in your mind.

Elements of the Trade Summary   Here you will want to be able to get a quick snapshot of how you are doing. For each week, month, and campaign traded, record:

- Largest win/largest loss.
- Average win/average loss.
- Aggregate win/aggregate loss.

I like to record values in both pips and dollars.

If you use market environments, note the values (directional movement and volatility) for each trade.

The Daily and Weekly Trade Plan

One of the factors separating the winners from the losers in trading is that the winners conceptualize the future. That means they plan for contingencies, both good and bad. The markets move quickly, and in FOREX the leverage magnifies mistakes, making them costly. It's important to have contingency plans for all possible outcomes.

Much depends on your specific codex. In the most general terms, the prepared trader has plans for how the market evolves over any given trading session. See Figure 14.1.

A prime example of conceptualizing the future is anticipating the different forms a wave may propagate. The trader always wants to be prepared for all contingencies, not just the one he hopes will occur.

Your daily and weekly plans should also note which markets you are watching and which stage of the codex process each is in at the beginning and end of the session. The watchword is: Be prepared.

Design your plan according to the requirements of your own codex. Don't make it too long or involved. Its purpose is to keep you focused and on

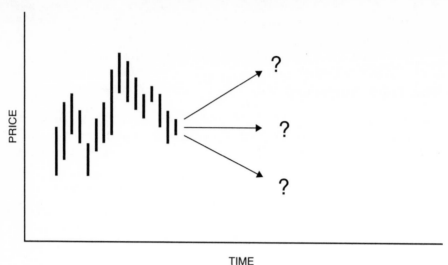

FIGURE 14.1   Conceptualizing the Future.
At minimum, go into each trading session with plans for what to do if the market moves sideways, up, or down.

track. I like to do my daily plan right after a session closes, and then review it before the next session begins.

Elements of the Trade Plan   The daily trade plan should be a short paragraph including the salient points you intend to observe. For example, does the 50 percent return price point constitute a continuation or reversal point? It should also include the times of any news or reports that will impact your trade. (How does the market react?) Any important contingencies should also be in the daily trade plan.

The trade plan serves to keep you focused, remind you of the critical factors in a trade, and allow you to make quick but intelligent decisions.

Diary

I also keep a short diary, separate from other reports, in a spiral binder. I make a short note before the session begins and a short note after it closes. This is where I try to keep track of my emotional state of being.

A diary entry need only be one or two sentences, before and after a trading session and after a trade has been exited. Its purpose is mostly to help you recall the trade later when you are reviewing your performance. For example, "I traded this EUR/USD off a 50 percent return. My profit objective was too close as the trade ran 40 pips past it."

If you use the Rogers Method (see the next section), you will need to store your diary on a CD or in a computer file.

The critical issue of a diary and summary is whether you can look at them a week or a month or even a year later and accurately take yourself back to that moment in time. Develop and use a consistent set of symbols and/or keyword terms.

The Rogers Method

Trader Joe Rogers, my friend, takes reports and feedback to the next level. I think it is an excellent idea, especially for the beginner and intermediate trader. Joe uses a product called Camtasia (www.techsmith.com) to fully record his trading sessions. The Rogers Method really doesn't take that much more time, but it does require an investment in time to set it up and learn it. It allows you to record all of your trading session, including the trading screen and even a webcam video of you. The product has a number of other useful features, as well, for archiving and annotating your session.

Techsmith also makes a nice utility called SnagIt that is great for annotating your charts.

Thanks to Joe Rogers for sharing the Camtasia method with me!

Summary

It takes time to do even modest reports, and it takes effort to do them consistently. No one likes to think about a trade gone bad, but those are the most important ones to track. You learn more from your losses than from your wins.

A single report may not provide you with much feedback or useful information. It is in the longer-term log of many trades that you will see patterns of behavior useful to honing your process and your trading skills.

15

Options and Options

Gentlemen don't trade oats—or options.

—Charles B. Goodman

lthough the money management and style concepts in this book should be adequate for all traders, you may want to explore other ideas for your toolbox of trading techniques.

As I mentioned early in the book, the sheer number of technical trading ideas is enormous; it is not uncommon for a trader to quite literally get lost in the process of exploration. Be careful. You can prune the materials to some extent simply by eliminating those that do not appeal to you or that do not fit your trading style or codex.

My advice is, as always, keep it simple!

Trading Tools

Following is a brief discussion of some popular trading tools and where to look for more information.

Candlestick charts. These have proven very popular with FOREX traders. There are any number of identified short-term patterns, and with further study you may find others applicable to currency trading. A serious statistical study of these patterns and their reliability would be useful. Pending that, I recommend the *bathtub analysis* approach mentioned in Chapter 6.

Almost all FOREX trading stations offer candlestick charts. The guru of candlestick charting is Steve Nison. His *Japanese Candlestick Charting*, published by the New York Institute of Finance (1991), is the basic primer.

Joe Ross. Joe Ross has written three books on commodity futures trading, primarily using short-term bar chart techniques: *Trading by the Minute, Trading the Ross Hook,* and *Trading by the Book,* all published by the author (http://.tradingeducators.com).

DiNapoli Levels. Some traders swear by DiNapoli Levels. I find the entire concept a bit subjective, as I do Elliott Wave and Gann theory, but you might find the concept a potential addition to your toolbox. I recommend *Trading with DiNapoli Levels,* published by Coast Investment Software (1997).

Classic bar charts. The classic bar chart patterns have been around for decades and many traders still rely on them. Again, I find them too subjective. It is easy to see the patterns such as head-and-shoulders and pennants after the fact. Two books with information on these are Robert Edwards and John McKee's *Technical Analysis of Stock Trends* (1948) and Thomas Bulkowski's *Encyclopedia of Chart Patterns* (New York: Wiley Trading, 2000). Another resource is *Trading Commodity Futures with Classical Chart Patterns,* by Peter Brandt (1990).

    Charts are charts. A book emphasizing stock charts or commodity futures charts is perfectly fine for the FOREX trader as a study guide to the technique in question.

Point and figure charting. Although P&F charts have fallen in popularity, they are still an excellent way to record and analyze prices. My favorite books on point and figure charting are *The Point and Figure Method of Anticipating Stock Price Movements,* by Victor De Villiers and Owen Taylor; *The Three-Point Reversal Method of Point and Figure,* by A. W. Cohen; and *Point and Figure Charting: The Complete Guide,* by Carroll Aby.

Taylor and the old school. Before the advent of computer analysis—mostly in the 1940s, 1950s, and 1960s—a great number of books were printed on charting techniques. Many of these were privately printed in small quantities and are almost impossible to obtain today, such as Burton Pugh's *The Great Wheat Secret.* Fortunately, Ed Dobson's Traders Press (www.traderspress.com) has seen fit to reprint some of them. They are certainly worth exploring. One I have found useful is *The Taylor Trading Technique,* by George Taylor.

Indicators. If you want to study or use indicators despite my caveats and reservations, the seminal work is Welles Wilder's *New Concepts in Technical Trading Techniques.*

Volume and open interest. Because there is no central clearinghouse or reporting agency, there are no volume or open interest figures for currency trading. This is a shame, because they are very useful to the commodity futures trader. There are a number of excellent works about volume and open interest, including *Charting Commodity Market Price Behavior*, by Lee Belveal; *Volume Cycles in the Stock Market*, by Richard Arms; and *Volume and Open Interest*, by Kenneth Shaleen.

I am currently working on formulas for deriving synthetic FOREX volume and open interest. I will publish my findings on my web site, www.fxpraxis.com. Once established, they will allow the FOREX trader to use the same tools as does the commodity futures trader.

The Companion *volumes.* These books, eight in number and directed to the FOREX trader, were privately published by this author and James Bickford. They offer a plethora of new ideas and statistical analysis for the currency trader. The *FOREX Chartist Companion* volume, with substantial updating, has been republished by John Wiley & Sons.

The Internet. If you Google "technical analysis" and related keywords and terms such as "FOREX trading techniques" or "market trading systems," you will find hundreds of web sites with many interesting trading techniques, methods, and systems. Other popular ideas you can explore with an Internet search: Bollinger Bands, Gann theory, and Elliott Wave theory.

Options

Options for stocks have been around for more than 100 years. Listed or regularly traded options for stocks and commodity futures have been available to traders since the 1970s. However, options are new to FOREX and are definitely worth exploring.

I recommend options as a money management technique and *not* as a primary trading vehicle. Option theory can be enormously complex mathematically, but if you stay with the basic ideas you might find them a worthy addition to your codex. If you Google "option trading," you will find many primers and in-depth resource guides on the Internet.

What Is an Option?

An *option* is the right to buy or sell something at a specific price for a specific period of time. Buying an option is essentially buying time.

One advantage of buying an option is that your loss is limited by the price you paid for the option; you can never lose more than that amount.

Option Terms

At-the-money.

An option is at-the-money if the strike price of the option is equal to the market price of the underlying security.

Call. An option contract that gives the holder the right to buy the underlying security at a specified price for a certain fixed period of time.

Put. An option contract that gives the holder the right to sell the underlying security at a specified price for a certain fixed period of time.

Strike Price. The stated price per share for which the underlying security may be purchased (in the case of a call) or sold (in the case of a put) by the option holder upon exercise of the option contract.

Time Decay. A term used to describe how the theoretical value of an option "erodes" or reduces with the passage of time.

Both www.cboe.com and www.phlx.com have complete glossaries of options terms.

Courtesy www.CBOE.com.

Types of Options

Principally, there are two types of options. The right to buy is a *call*. The right to sell is a *put*. You are said to have the right to "call" the stock, commodity future, or currency if you purchase a call. You are said to have the right to "put" the stock, commodity future, or currency if you buy a put.

Puts and Calls

A call is the right to purchase the underlying long currency. A put is the right to sell the underlying long currency. In FOREX, this essentially means being long the other currency in the pair or cross.

Of course, someone must give you that right to call or put. That person is the other side of your options contract and is termed the *writer*. As a FOREX trader, you may consider being either a buyer of put and call options or a writer. Buying is simpler and more common. Writing and its various permutations can become complicated and should be considered only by the trader with substantial market experience.

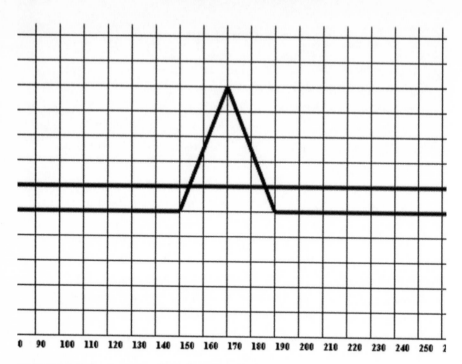

| 0 | 90 | 100 | 110 | 120 | 130 | 140 | 150 | 160 | 170 | 180 | 190 | 200 | 210 | 220 | 230 | 240 | 250 | 2 |

FIGURE 15.1 Complex Option Strategies.
You may either *buy* (purchase) calls or puts or you may *write* calls or puts. Writing options is beyond the scope of this book but involves many complex strategies that appeal to advanced traders. Exotic strategies involve combinations of puts and calls as well as both buying and writing. They often have names based on the visual outline of the strategy. Writing may also be used as a money management tool.

Complex strategies with esoteric names such as *butterfly* and *condor* refer to simultaneous buying and writing of calls and puts for different strikes and exercise prices. These are definitely best left to the options specialist! See Figure 15.1.

Options for Money Management

As a money management technique, buying calls and puts may serve as an insurance policy on your trade. Typically, they work best if you plan to hold a trade for some period of time, which is not a common prospect for the currency trader.

An insurance policy protects you against the opposite outcome from what you expect or desire. If you buy life insurance, it protects your heirs if you die.

If you are long a currency against another currency—for example, EUR/USD, where you are long the dollar—you may purchase a USD put against the EUR as protection. If your stop is hit or the market goes against you, your losses are mitigated by the profit in your put.

If you are short a currency against another currency—for example, the EUR/USD, where you are short the dollar—you may purchase a USD call against the EUR as protection. If your stop is hit or the market goes against you, your losses are mitigated by the profit in your call.

It sounds wonderful, doesn't it? Unfortunately, calls and puts cost money; the cost of an option goes to the writer for giving you the calling or putting rights. You must calculate the cost of your option against the value of the insurance protection. Sometimes it works out to your advantage, but often it does not—primarily because of the cost.

When buying an option, you are paying for the time. The more time you purchase, the higher the cost. As the market moves, that time gets shorter and shorter. The time value of an option is said to *decay*. My experience is that this decay is very difficult to calculate in advance. See Figure 15.2.

The closer your option is to the strike price, the more expensive it will be, as well.

The twin factors of decaying time and fluctuating prices of the underlying instrument make options pricing very difficult. You can win but still lose.

Win and Lose

It is not uncommon for the options trader to apparently win and yet lose. The price of a currency may go in the direction, generating an underlying price profit. But the time value may erode at a faster rate, causing the value of the option to fall, not rise.

To win, the price profit in an option must increase at a greater rate than the rate at which the time value decays.

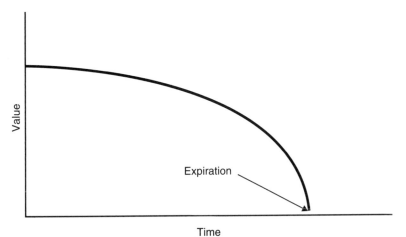

FIGURE 15.2 Options Decay.

I do not recommend trading options as a substitute for cash or spot FOREX. Other than the slight carrying charges for spot currencies, very little cost is involved beyond the bid-ask spread. I've also found that options tend to make a trader lazy and lax. Because your loss in buying a put or call is limited to the price you paid, its value can only go to zero. Inexperienced traders tend to put off decisions from one day to the next, only to see the option expire, worthless, and their money lost.

Caution: If you trade or use options, trade *only* with a reliable broker/dealer or options exchange. The Commodity Futures Trading Commission (CFTC) and the National Futures Association (NFA) have logged hundreds of complaints from people who have been swindled by options from disreputable dealers or "boiler shops."

The Philadelphia Options Exchange

The Philadelphia Options Exchange (PHLX) has recently introduced options on FOREX. The number of options is quite limited at this time (see Table 15.1). Listed stock options trading began in the 1970s with very few options, and now thousands are offered. I expect a similar course in listed FOREX options as professional traders and hedge funds accept them as a legitimate trading tool. The PHLX (Philadelphia Options Exchange) has been in business for many years and has an excellent reputation. Go to www.phlx.com for more information, including excellent educational resources.

	AUD	GBP	CAD	EUR	JPY	CHF	USD
TABLE 15.1 PHLX Options							
AUD	1	0.4103	0.9319	0.6048	95.2300	0.9823	0.8086
GBP	2.4338	1	2.2708	1.4731	231.8200	2.3916	1.9673
CAD	1.0731	0.4404	1	0.6491	102.0700	1.0530	0.8661
EUR	1.6510	0.6786	1.5407	1	157.3400	1.6229	1.3350
JPY	0.0105	0.0043	0.0098	0.0063	1	0.0103	0.0084
CHF	1.0177	0.4182	0.9492	0.6163	96.9100	1	0.8221
USD	1.2367	0.5083	1.1528	0.7491	117.8200	1.2152	1

Source: www.PHLX.com.

Box Options

FOREX brokers and dealers are also beginning to offer options. The optimum strategy is, of course, to trade both spot currencies and FOREX under the same roof. The logistics of doing otherwise may be very difficult, if not impossible in some cases.

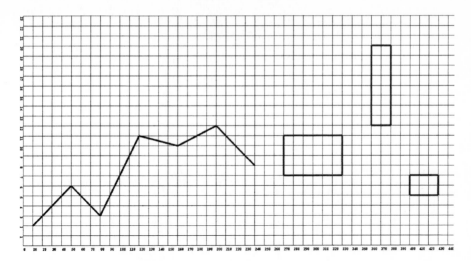

FIGURE 15.3 Box Options.

A FOREX broker-dealer, OANDA Corporation (www.oanda.com), now offers *box options*. These are preset options packages. They are called box options because you are trading in a box defined by time and price variables.

OANDA's parameters for their box options are not in the public domain, so to some extent you are trading blind. Nonetheless, they are quite interesting and open up any number of opportunities for the FOREX trader. See Figure 15.3. (It is probably possible to reverse-engineer the OANDA box option parameters, given enough sample trades. This may or may not be valuable information insofar as the broker/dealer might simply reset the parameters at any time.)

Summary

I recommend options as a money management tool only to intermediate traders and up. Be comfortable with your trading method before considering options. The same can be said for adding any new trading tools to your codex. If you are a position trader, options most definitely bear consideration. Options writing and complex strategies should be left to the advanced trader and professionals. I do not recommend trading options as your primary vehicle, in place of spot FOREX.

It's fun and exciting to explore the world of technical analysis. But it can become an addiction and a detriment to your trading. Don't add a technique to your codex unless you are very comfortable with using it and you understand clearly what it does and what it actually measures.

Many are the traders who have lost the forest for the trees in the pursuit of technical analysis.

16

The Dreams of Reason— To Be or Not to Be a FOREX Trader

Walking away is better than being carried out.

—Charles B. Goodman

Will you wave a currency trader's checkered flag or a white towel? FOREX trading is great fun. It can also be very profitable. But the reality is, it is not for everyone. There may be many reasons traders fail at FOREX. Some are common and correctible. It is worth reviewing the characteristics of a successful trader from *Getting Started in Currency Trading*.

Nine Characteristics of Successful Traders

1. Successful traders tend to have absolute control over their emotions—they never get too elated over a win or too depressed over a loss.

2. Successful traders seldom think of prices as "too high" or "too low."

3. Successful traders do not panic. They make evolutionary adjustments rather than revolutionary changes to their trading style.

4. Successful traders do not flinch at making the decision to take a loss, never let losses ride, and never add to losing trades. One old trader told me he thought of his positions as stock in a retail store. If

something sells and is making you money, you add to that line. If something is not selling and it's costing you money, you discount it and unload it as quickly as possible.

5. Successful traders treat trading as business and not a hobby.

6. Successful traders stay physically fit.

7. Successful traders are prepared for all eventualities on any given trading day. They come to work with a plan that includes many contingencies and not just what they hope will happen. In your own trading program you should have predetermined answers to "What happens if . . ." prices open sharply higher or lower, the market is very quiet, the market is very volatile, the market makes new highs, the market makes new lows, the market goes up early and reverses later, the market goes down early and reverses later.

8. Successful traders trade only with money they can afford to lose. Trading FOREX is speculative and can result in substantial loss. It is also exciting, exhilarating, and can be addictive. The more you are emotionally involved with your money, the harder it is to make objective, clearheaded decisions about market entry and exit.

9. Successful traders adapt to change but never panic.

Sadly, we cannot all be winners. There are no specific statistics on FOREX trading, mostly because there is no centralized clearing or recording mechanism. But I think it is safe to assume that the statistics in FOREX are not different from those in commodity futures where leverage is also the name of the game. In futures, it is estimated that 90 percent lose and 10 percent win. Not very democratic, but certainly a boon for the 10 percent winners.

If you consistently lose money at FOREX, even after diligently doing everything possible to win, what's wrong? No simple answer exists, obviously, or we would all be winners, and the markets would cease to exist. But the issue may be divided into two categories: emotions and abilities.

Emotions

You may not be emotionally cut out to be a trader. Because of the leverage in FOREX, mistakes are enormously magnified and quickly make themselves felt. Emotional weakness is harshly penalized. Greed and fear, fear and greed—some of us are better able to control them than others.

The best advice I can offer is to start trading very small amounts of money and very small trade lot sizes. Begin trading a demo account, then move on to a mini or micro account. Trade progressively as you demonstrate success in lot sizes of $100, $500, $1,000, $10,000, $25,000, and so forth, up to the limits of your money management parameters.

At some point you will notice either a demonstrable fall in your winning percentages and/or emotional confusion or angst. Drop down one level and stay there for a few months. Then try progressing again. The markets will not go away; time is on your side.

Abilities

It is a mystery why some people excel at some tasks and others, with equal or superior intelligence, fail. Consider the game of chess. I've played chess for almost 40 years, and although I have attained a lower degree of competence—an "Expert" rating—it is abundantly clear, despite hundreds of hours of study, I will never succeed at the game in any big way.

In chess, the theory is that your brain is either wired for the tasks it demands, primarily visualization skills, or it is not. If you are wired correctly, you play good chess, study or no study. This explains the existence of child prodigies such as Capablanca and Reshevsky. World champion Garry Kasparov refers to it as the "chess geometry" ability.

Trading may have a similar paradigm. There is probably a neural wiring, or at least a set of least innate traits or propensities, determining success or failure in the markets.

I've certainly seen some very smart people try very hard, work extremely diligently, and still go bust in short order. I've also seen, less frequently, people take to trading as if it were as natural as talking. What those traits or propensities might be, I do not know. But without them, long-term success may be difficult to achieve.

Some of the best traders seem to have few skills outside the trading arena; trading is truly their life. Bill Gates is the world's richest man, but no one who has heard him speak without notes would accuse him of being the sharpest knife in the drawer!

It's possible you can develop those traits to some degree; I have tried to assist you in that with this book. But without the wiring, only so much may be possible. An acorn becomes an oak tree, not a blueberry bush.

Develop a simple codex. Emphasize money management and style over trading tools. Remember what Charlie said: "The markets can only go up or down." Don't make it complicated simply because it is possible to have a battery of 37 different technical indicators. With a simple trading plan, errors are more easily seen and analyzed, and adjustments can be made to a simple plan much more easily than to a complex one.

If you've failed only marginally at FOREX and have the determination and money, keep trying. But if you go down in flames in one trading campaign after the other, it may be time to wave the white towel and move on to another area more fitting to your emotional makeup, your specific traits, or your wiring.

One More Time

If your FOREX venture has failed, but you are willing to try one more time, take the following steps:

1. Take a month off and don't look at or think about the FOREX markets.

2. Take the next week to make a list of what you think went wrong. Make corrections and aim to greatly simplify your trade plan.

3. Adjust your trade plan accordingly.

4. Allocate your capital using the campaign method in Part One.

5. Trade your most successful currency pair and no others for 30 days.

I wish you success in FOREX trading and in all life's endeavors.

Visual Basic Source Code

O ver the years, I have written numerous trading programs and backtest-ing utilities for commodity futures and currencies. The following Microsoft Visual Basic 6.0 source code outlines a program I designed to calculate moving directional movement and volatility indexes for market environments; the code was written by my colleague James Bickford as part of a larger programming task.

```
Public Type QUOTE_TYPE
   Date As Date
   Time As String
   O As Double
   H As Double
   L As Double
   C As Double
End Type
Public Q(MAXQUOTES) As QUOTE_TYPE

Public Sub CalculateDM(DMIdx%)
Dim i%
   For i = DMIdx + 1 To NumQuotes
     DM(i) = Q(i).C - Q(i - DMIDX).C
   Next i
End Sub
```

```
Public Sub CalculateVolatility(VolIdx%)
Dim i%, j%
Dim sum#, mean#
  sum = 0
  For i = VolIdx To NumQuotes
    sum = 0
    For j = i - VolIdx + 1 To i
      sum = sum + Q(j).C
    Next j
    mean = sum / VolIdx
    sum = 0
    For j = i - VolIdx + 1 To i
      sum = sum + Abs(Q(i).C - mean)
    Next j
    Vol(i) = sum / VolIdx
  Next i
End Sub
```

The block of code to calculate the impact ratio follows:

```
Public Sub CalculateImpact(ImpactIdx%)
Dim i%

  For i = 1 To NumQuotes
    Impact(i) = 100 * Abs((Q(i).C - Q(i).O)) /
(Q(i).H - Q(i).L)
  Next i


End Sub
```

How the FOREX Game
Is Played

There are two types of retail FOREX brokers: market makers and electronic communications networks (ECNs).

An ECN works similarly to how the interbank foreign exchange market works. Orders are matched on a client-to-client basis. A large network of banks, institutions, and traders connect to the network and orders are matched; there is no central clearinghouse for orders. If you wish to sell 50 million U.S. dollars (USD) dollars against the euro (EUR), you place your order and wait for someone who wants to buy. Typically, because of the huge volume of foreign exchange business, transactions are instantaneous. The market is said to be *liquid*. Nevertheless, your order technically requires a counterparty to be executed.

ECN retail FOREX brokers build their own network and often tap into the interbank ECN.

Market Maker or ECN?

Most retail brokers, especially the smaller ones accepting so-called mini accounts, are market makers. Market makers act as a de facto central clearinghouse for their clients. If you look closely at market maker web sites and their account documentation, you will see a statement such as, "XYZ-FOREX is the counterparty to all trades."

Market makers typically guarantee execution at the price you want, assuming their data stream touches that price. There are exceptions, however, as I discuss here.

Market makers sometimes trade against their own clients. There is inherently nothing wrong with this; that is how they play the game. Trading against their clients performs three useful functions: (1) It provides liquidity, (2) it helps maintain an orderly market, and (3) it keeps their book from becoming too unbalanced. Because they are the counterparty to all trades, if they have 500 million USD on the buy side and only 50 million USD on the sell side (this is an exaggeration to make the point—balance is rarely off more than 5 percent), market makers are at risk if the USD should fall sharply. Market makers often hand off large orders to an ECN or the interbank market to maintain balance.

Market makers are effectively bookmakers. In choosing a market maker broker, it is good to know how much net worth or liquidity they have in case they do suffer from an order imbalance. The Commodity Futures Trading Commission (CFTC) is working to set minimum net worth/liquidity requirements for market makers. But this is a work in progress, and FOREX today remains very much a *caveat emptor* enterprise.

Market makers have been known to "requote" prices—executing an order that does not show on their price feed. This is also known as "dealer intervention" and is the number-one complaint traders have with market makers in FOREX.

Market makers are often accused of *running* or *harvesting* stop-loss orders. To a limited extent this is in pursuit of the three legitimate functions listed earlier. However, if a broker/dealer harvests stops primarily as a profit center, traders are not happy. It is very difficult, if not impossible, to tell if a market maker is running stops at all and, if they are, the motive. Such is the capitalist experience. Because of the lax regulatory environment the inner workings of retail brokers are more opaque than they are transparent.

(If you have access to multiple data streams you can watch for stop harvesting. If one of the streams shows a sharp price spike, resulting in a price several pips from the maximum or minimum of all the other streams, it is possibly a case of stop harvesting, especially if it is in an active market with good liquidity.)

FOREX markets are said to be "fast" especially after the release of a major news announcement. This means there is a dramatic increase in price movement and/or volatility. Market makers often dramatically increase their pip spreads (*ballooning*) for a short period of time under these conditions to maintain order balance. Pip spreads have been know to balloon from 2 pips to as much as 30 pips for one or two minutes after a Federal Reserve announcement. There are horror stories of ballooning 100 to 200 pips. Spreads also balloon during inactive market periods when liquidity is low. Traders should either avoid trading during these times or at least be aware of this phenomenon. Ballooning spreads should be a legitimate market maker function, but many traders believe some market makers use it as a profit center technique. Again, *caveat emptor.*

If you *trade the News*—and I recommend against it for the beginning trader—use an execution tool such as www.secretnewsweapon.com.

Even on an ECN platform, executions in fast markets may be off your price by many pips. A 5-pip slippage might not dramatically affect a day trader or a position trader, but it is a very significant cost to the guerilla trader or the scalper.

At the highest level of foreign exchange trading there are two games being played simultaneously. The first is simply attempting to determine what prices are going to do. There is a second, tactical level, less visible but very real.

The tactical level demands that the trader (1) know what the other players are doing or planning to do; (2) keep the other players from knowing what you are going to do; and, perhaps most interesting, (3) feed the other players false information so their conclusions about what you are going to do or planning to do are incorrect. The typical retail FOREX trader need not concern himself with this tactical level but should be aware of its existence.

Most of the order execution issues of interest to the retail FOREX trader stem from the fact there is no central clearinghouse for currency trading.

Many web sites offer broker/dealer reviews. When reading these reviews keep four points in mind: (1) Satisfied traders generally post less than unsatisfied traders; (2) the larger the broker/dealer, the larger its volume of complaints; (3) a small sample of reviews may not be meaningful; and (4) seeing similar complaints on multiple web sites increase the chances of the complaints being legitimate.

For reviews check out www.forexbastards.com, www.moneytec.com, www.goforex.com, www.forex-ratings.com, and www.forexreview.org. For others, Google "FOREX broker reviews," "currency dealer reviews," "FOREX broker complaints," and permutations thereof.

Glossary

algorithmic trading   Trading by means of an automated computer program; sometimes called *program trading.*

application program interface (API)   Computer code or routines for integrating trading programs to a broker/dealer's trading platform. Most commonly used to allow a proprietary trading program to read and process a broker/dealer's data feed.

appreciation   A currency is said to appreciate when it strengthens in price in response to market demand.

arbitrage   The purchase or sale of an instrument and simultaneous taking of an equal and opposite position in a related market, in order to take advantage of small price differentials between markets.

ask price   The price at which the market is prepared to sell a specific currency in a foreign exchange contract or cross currency contract. At this price, the trader can buy the base currency. The ask price is shown on the right side of the quotation. For example, in the quote "USD/CHF 1.4527/32," the ask price is 1.4532, meaning you can buy one U.S. dollar for 1.4532 Swiss francs.

at best   An instruction given to a dealer to buy or sell at the best rate that can be obtained.

at or better   An order to deal at a specific rate or better.

balance of trade   The value of a country's exports minus its imports.

ballooning   The practice by market makers of increasing pip spreads during fast or illiquid markets.

bar chart   A type of chart that consists of four significant points: the high and the low prices, which form the vertical bar; the opening price, which is marked with a little horizontal line to the left of the bar; and the closing price, which is marked with a little horizontal line to the right of the bar.

base currency   The first currency in a currency pair. It shows how much the base currency is worth as measured against the second currency. For example, if the USD/CHF rate equals 1.6215 then one USD is worth CHF 1.6215. In the foreign exchange markets, the U.S. dollar is normally considered the base currency for quotes, meaning that quotes are expressed as a unit of $1 (USD) per the other currency quoted in the pair. The primary exceptions to this rule are the British pound (GBP), the euro (EUR), and the Australian dollar (AUD).

bear market   A market distinguished by declining prices.

bid price   The price at which the market is prepared to buy a specific currency in a foreign exchange contract or cross currency contract. At this price, the trader can sell the base currency. It is shown on the left side of the quotation. For example, in the quote "USD/CHF 1.4527/32," the bid price is 1.4527, meaning you can sell one U.S. dollar for 1.4527 Swiss francs.

bid/ask spread   The difference between the bid and offer price.

big figure quote   Dealer expression referring to the first few digits of an exchange rate. These digits are often omitted in dealer quotes. For example, a USD/JPY rate might be 117.30/117.35, but would be quoted verbally without the first three digits, that is, "30/35."

BLS   Bureau of Labor Statistics.

book   In a professional trading environment, a book is the summary of a trader's or desk's total positions.

broker   An individual or firm that acts as an intermediary, putting together buyers and sellers for a fee or commission. In contrast, a *dealer* commits capital and takes one side of a position, hoping to earn a spread (profit) by closing out the position in a subsequent trade with another party.

Bretton Woods Agreement of 1944   An agreement that established fixed foreign exchange rates for major currencies, provided for central bank intervention in the currency markets, and pegged the price of gold at US $35 per ounce. The agreement lasted until 1971, when President Nixon overturned the Bretton Woods Agreement and established a floating exchange rate for the major currencies.

bull market   A market distinguished by rising prices.

Bundesbank   Germany's central bank.

cable   Trader jargon referring to the sterling/U.S. dollar exchange rate. So called because the rate was originally transmitted via a transatlantic cable beginning in the mid-1800s.

call   An option to purchase a currency.

cambist   An expert trader who rapidly buys and sells currency throughout the day.

candlestick chart   A chart that indicates the trading range for the day as well as the opening and closing price. If the open price is higher than the close price, the rectangle between the two is shaded. If the close price is higher than the open price, that area of the chart is not shaded.

cash market   The market in the actual financial instrument on which a futures or options contract is based.

central bank   A government or quasi-governmental organization that manages a country's monetary policy. For example, the U.S. central bank is the Federal Reserve, and the German central bank is the Bundesbank.

centralized market   Any market where all orders routed to one central exchange. FOREX is not a centralized market.

CFTC   Commodity Futures Trading Commission.

chartist An individual who uses charts and graphs and interprets historical data to find trends and predict future movements. Also referred to as *technical trader.*

cleared funds Funds that are freely available, sent in to settle a trade.

closed position Exposures in foreign currencies that no longer exist. The process to close a position is to sell or buy a certain amount of currency to offset an equal amount of the open position. This will square the position.

clearing The process of settling a trade.

CME Chicago Mercantile Exchange.

consumer price index (CPI) A weighted average of prices of a basket of consumer goods and services, such as food, medical, and transportation. The CPI is calculated by taking price changes for each item in a specified basket of goods and averaging them according to their estimated importance.

contagion The tendency of an economic crisis to spread from one market to another. In 1997, political instability in Indonesia caused high volatility in their domestic currency, the rupiah. From there, the contagion spread to other Asian emerging currencies, and then to Latin America, and is now referred to as the *Asian contagion.*

collateral Something given to secure a loan or as a guarantee of performance.

commission A transaction fee charged by a broker.

confirmation A document exchanged by counterparts to a transaction that states the terms of said transaction.

contract The standard unit of trading in futures and options.

counter currency The second listed currency in a currency pair. See also *quote currency.*

counterparty One of the participants in a financial transaction.

country risk Risk associated with a cross-border transaction, including but not limited to legal and political conditions.

cross currency pair A foreign exchange transaction in which one foreign currency is traded against a second foreign currency—for example, EUR/GBP.

cross rate Same as *cross currency pair.*

currency Any form of money issued by a government or central bank and used as legal tender and a basis for trade.

currency pair The two currencies that make up a foreign exchange rate. For example, EUR/USD.

currency risk The probability of an adverse change in exchange rates.

day trader A speculator who takes positions in currencies, which are then liquidated prior to the close of the same trading session or day.

dealer An individual or firm that acts as a principal or counterpart to a transaction. Principals take one side of a position, hoping to earn a spread (profit) by closing out the position in a subsequent trade with another party. In contrast, a broker is an individual or firm that acts as an intermediary, putting together buyers and sellers for a fee or commission.

deficit   A negative balance of trade or payments.

delivery   A FOREX trade where both sides make and take actual delivery of the currencies traded.

depreciation   A fall in the value of a currency due to market forces.

derivative   A contract that changes in value in relation to the price movements of a related or underlying security, future, or other physical instrument. An option is the most common derivative instrument.

devaluation   The deliberate downward adjustment of a currency's price, normally by official announcement.

directional movement   In technical analysis, the net price change from one specified time unit to another specified time unit. See also *volatility*.

downtick   A new price quote at a price lower than the preceding quote.

econometric analysis   The use of mathematical formulas or models to make trading decisions with fundamental information and data.

economic indicator   A government-issued statistic that indicates current economic growth and stability. Common indicators include employment rates, gross domestic product (GDP), inflation, retail sales, and so forth.

electronic communications network (ECN)   A system wherein orders to buy and sell are matched through a network of banks and/or dealers. See *market maker*, the other widely used method of order execution, and *NDD*, a hybrid.

European currency unit (ECU)   See *European Monetary Union (EMU)*.

end of day order (EOD)   An order to buy or sell at a specified price. This order remains open until the end of the trading day, which is typically 5:00 P.M. Eastern time.

European Monetary Union (EMU)   The principal goal of the EMU was to establish a single European currency called the *euro*, which officially replaced the national currencies of the member EU countries in 2002. On January 1, 1999, the transitional phase to introduce the euro began. The euro now exists as a banking currency, and paper financial transactions and foreign exchange are made in euros. This transition period lasted for three years, at which time euro notes and coins entered circulation. As of July 1, 2002, only euros are legal tender for EMU participants, and the national currencies of the member countries have ceased to exist. The current members of the EMU (as of March 2007) are Austria, Belgium, Finland, France, Germany, Greece, Ireland, Italy, Luxembourg, the Netherlands, Portugal, Slovenia, and Spain.

euro   the currency of the European Monetary Union (EMU). A replacement for the European Currency Unit (ECU).

European Central Bank (ECB)   The central bank for the new European Monetary Union.

exotics   A currency pair with the USD and a lesser-traded currency such as the Thai baht or the Chilean peso; considered riskier to trade than the *majors* or *minors*.

fast market   A market is fast when it is hit with a large volume of orders over a short period of time. Markets are often fast after an unexpected news announcement.

Federal Deposit Insurance Corporation (FDIC)   The regulatory agency responsible for administering bank depository insurance in the United States.

Federal Reserve (Fed)   The central bank for the United States.

first in, first out (FIFO)   Open positions are closed according to the FIFO accounting rule. All positions opened within a particular currency pair are liquidated in the order in which they were originally opened.

flat/square   A trader on the sidelines with no position.

floating stop   An automated *trailing stop*.

foreign exchange (FOREX, FX)   The simultaneous buying of one currency and selling of another.

FOREX futures   FOREX traded as a futures contract.

forward   The prespecified exchange rate for a foreign exchange contract settling at some agreed future date, based on the interest rate differential between the two currencies involved.

forward points   The pips added to or subtracted from the current exchange rate to calculate a forward price.

fundamental analysis   Analysis of economic and political information with the objective of determining future movements in a financial market.

futures contract   An obligation to exchange a good or instrument at a set price on a future date. The primary difference between a future and a forward is that futures are typically traded over an exchange (exchange-traded contracts, or ETC), versus forwards, which are considered over-the-counter (OTC) contracts. An OTC is any contract *not* traded on an exchange.

FX   Foreign exchange.

G8   The eight leading industrial countries, namely the United States, Germany, Japan, France, the United Kingdom, Canada, Italy, and Russia.

going long   The purchase of a stock, commodity, or currency for investment or speculation.

going short   The selling of a currency or instrument not owned by the seller.

gold standard   A monetary system whereby a country allows its monetary unit to be freely converted into fixed amounts of gold and vice versa.

gross domestic product (GDP)   Total value of a country's output, income, or expenditure produced within the country's physical borders.

gross national product (GNP)   Gross domestic product plus income earned from investment or work abroad.

good till cancelled order (GTC)   An order to buy or sell at a specified price. This order remains open until filled or until the client cancels.

guerilla trader Similar to a scalper, but a guerilla trades in bursts with a flurry of trades and then quickly retreats to the sidelines; also called a sniper.

hedge A position or combination of positions that reduces the risk of your primary position.

high-frequency trading Trading very frequently; scalping. See *ultra high frequency trading*.

hit the bid Acceptance of purchasing at the offer or selling at the bid.

inflation An economic condition whereby prices for consumer goods rise, eroding purchasing power.

initial margin The initial deposit of collateral required to enter into a position as a guarantee on future performance.

interbank rates The foreign exchange rates at which large international banks quote other large international banks.

intervention Action by a central bank to affect the value of its currency by entering the market. Concerted intervention refers to action by a number of central banks to control exchange rates.

introducing broker Generally a small broker who relies on a larger broker/dealer to execute his trades and hold fiduciary responsibility for client funds.

King Kong syndrome The emotional high that overtakes a trader when he does exceptionally well for a period of time, such as making a dozen consecutive winning trades. It is usually followed by a large losing trade and a reality check.

kiwi Slang for the New Zealand dollar.

leading indicators Statistics that are considered to predict future economic activity.

leverage Also called margin. The ratio of the amount used in a transaction to the required security deposit.

London Interbank Offered Rate (LIBOR) Banks use LIBOR when borrowing from another bank.

limit order An order with restrictions on the maximum price to be paid or the minimum price to be received. As an example, if the current price of USD/YEN is 117.00/05, then a limit order to buy USD would be at a price below 116.50.

liquidation The closing of an existing position through the execution of an offsetting transaction.

liquidity The ability of a market to accept large transactions with minimal to no impact on price stability; also the ability to enter and exit a market quickly.

long position A position that appreciates in value if market prices increase. When the base currency in the pair is bought, the position is said to be long.

loonie Slang for the Canadian dollar.

lot A unit to measure the amount of the deal. The value of the deal always corresponds to an integer number of lots.

major currency Any of the following: euro, pound sterling, Australian dollar, New Zealand dollar, U.S. dollar, Canadian dollar, Swiss franc, Japanese yen. See also *minor currency*.

managed account An account in which a third party such as a professional money manager makes trading decisions for you. Also called a discretionary account.

margin The required equity that an investor must deposit to collateralize a position.

margin call A request from a broker or dealer for additional funds or other collateral to guarantee performance on a position that has moved against the customer.

market maker A dealer who regularly quotes both bid and ask prices and is ready to make a two-sided market for any financial instrument. Most retail FOREX dealers are market makers. A market maker is said to have a dealing desk.

market risk Exposure to changes in market prices.

mark-to-market Process of reevaluating all open positions with the current market prices. These new values then determine margin requirements.

maturity The date for settlement or expiry of a financial instrument.

mercury chart A modified bar chart used in commodity futures. Each bar shows the price range for a time unit and changes in open interest and volume from the previous time unit.

minor currency Any of the currencies between a major currency and an exotic. The Italian lira and Swedish krona are minor currencies.

money management The techniques a trader utilizes to manage his money both in the aggregate and for specific trades.

money supply The aggregate quantity of coins, bills, loans, credit and any other liquid monetary instruments or equivalents within a given country's economy.

mundo A synthetic global currency calculated as the average of multiple ISO currency pairs. See Michael Archer and James Bickford, *FOREX Chartist Companion* (New York: John Wiley & Sons, 2006).

NDD A "no dealing desk" broker. Provides a platform where liquidity providers such as banks can offer prices; incoming orders are routed to the best available bid or offer. See also *market maker* and *electronic communications network (ECN)*.

net position The amount of currency bought or sold which has not yet been offset by opposite transactions.

NFA National Futures Association.

offer The rate at which a dealer is willing to sell a currency. See *ask price.*

offsetting transaction A trade that serves to cancel or offset some or all of the market risk of an open position.

one cancels the other order (OCO) A designation for two orders whereby when one part of the two orders is executed the other is automatically cancelled.

open order An order that will be executed when a market moves to its designated price. Normally associated with *good till cancelled* orders.

open position An active trade with corresponding unrealized profit and loss, which has not been offset by an equal and opposite deal.

option A FOREX option is the right to purchase or sell a currency at a specified price for a specified time period.

over-the-counter (OTC)   Used to describe any transaction that is not conducted over an exchange.

overnight position   A trade that remains open until the next business day.

order   An instruction to execute a trade at a specified rate.

pip   The smallest unit of price for any foreign currency. Digits added to or subtracted from the fourth decimal place, that is, 0.0001. Also called *points*.

point   100 pips.

point and figure charts   Similar to swing charts but using X's to denote upward-moving prices and O's to denote downward-moving prices.

political risk   Exposure to changes in governmental policy that will have an adverse effect on an investor's position.

position   An investor's netted total holdings of a given currency.

position trader   A trader who holds positions over multiple trading sessions.

premium   In the currency markets, describes the amount by which the forward or futures price exceeds the spot price.

pretzel chart   A price chart connecting the open, high, low, and close in such a fashion that it resembles a pretzel with two closed three-sided spaces connected through a center point.

price transparency   Describes quotes to which every market participant has equal access.

profit/loss (P/L) or gain/loss   The actual realized gain or loss resulting from trading activities on closed positions, plus the theoretical unrealized gain or loss on open positions that have been marked-to-market.

programmed trading   See *algorithmic trading*.

put   An option to sell a currency.

pyramiding   Adding to a position as the market moves up or down. Pyramiding a winning position is risky; pyramiding a losing position is suicide.

quote   An indicative market price, normally used for information purposes only.

quote currency   The second currency quoted in a FOREX currency pair. In a direct quote, the quote currency is the foreign currency itself. In an indirect quote, the quote currency is the domestic currency. See also *base currency* and *counter currency*.

rally   A recovery in price after a period of decline.

range   The difference between the highest and lowest price of a future recorded during a given trading session.

rate   The price of one currency in terms of another, typically used for dealing purposes.

requoting   The practice of a broker/dealer filling an order at a price not seen on their public price feed. Like *ballooning* and *running stops*, requoting is most typical of market makers and is frowned upon by traders. Also referred to as dealer intervention.

resistance level   A term used in technical analysis indicating a specific price level at which analysis concludes people will sell.

revaluation   An increase in the exchange rate for a currency as a result of central bank intervention. Opposite of *devaluation*.

risk   Exposure to uncertain change, most often used with a negative connotation of adverse change.

risk management   The employment of financial analysis and trading techniques to reduce and control exposure to various types of risk.

rollover   Process whereby the settlement of a deal is rolled forward to another value date. The cost of this process is based on the interest rate differential of the two currencies.

round trip   Buying and selling of a specified amount of currency.

running stops   The practice of market makers entering orders for the purpose of hitting customer stop-loss orders. Also called harvesting stops. Like *ballooning*, considered a negative practice by traders.

scalper   Someone who trades very often. Trades are typically measured in minutes but sometimes seconds.

settlement   The process by which a trade is entered into the books and records of the counterparts to a transaction. The settlement of currency trades may or may not involve the actual physical exchange of one currency for another.

short position   An investment position that benefits from a decline in market price. When the base currency in the pair is sold, the position is said to be short.

slippage   The difference in pips between the order price approved by the client and the price at which the order is actually executed.

spot price   The current market price. Settlement of spot transactions usually occurs within two business days.

spread   The difference between the bid and offer prices.

sterling   Slang for British pound.

stop-loss order   Order type whereby an open position is automatically liquidated at a specific price. Often used to minimize exposure to losses if the market moves against an investor's position. As an example, an investor who is long USD at 156.27 might wish to put in a stop-loss order for 155.49, which would limit losses should the dollar depreciate, possibly below 155.49.

support level   A technique used in technical analysis that indicates a specific price ceiling and floor at which a given exchange rate will automatically correct itself. Opposite of *resistance level*.

swap   A currency swap is the simultaneous sale and purchase of the same amount of a given currency at a forward exchange rate.

swing chart   A form of charting connecting prices filtered by a minimum increment. Similar to *point and figure charts*. Pugh swing charts use vertical lines connected by short horizontal lines. Line swing charts use angular lines connecting price to price. Swing charts are said to be price-functional; the time frame is not a parameter.

Swissy Market slang for Swiss franc.

technical analysis An effort to forecast prices by analyzing market data—that is, historical price trends and averages, volumes, open interest, and so forth.

tick A minimum change in time required for the price to change, up or down.

trading session The term most commonly means one of the three 8-hour sessions for trading FOREX over a 24-hour period: Asian, European, and North American. Technically there are five sessions between Sunday evening and Friday evening: The New York exchange trades from 7:30 A.M. to 5 P.M. EST. The Sydney, Auckland, and Wellington exchanges trade from 3 P.M. to 11 P.M. EST. The Tokyo exchange trades from 6 P.M. to 11 P.M., stopping for an hour-long lunch break and then trading again until 4 A.M. EST. The Hong Kong and Singapore exchanges trade from 7 P.M. to 3 A.M. EST. The last exchanges trading are the Munich, Zurich, Paris, Frankfurt, Brussels, Amsterdam, and London exchanges; these all trade from 2:30 A.M. to 11:30 A.M. EST.

trailing stop The practice of moving a stop-loss in the direction of the market's movement. Used primarily to protect profits. See also *floating stop*.

transaction cost The cost of buying or selling a financial instrument.

transaction date The date on which a trade occurs.

turnover The total money value of all executed transactions in a given time period; volume.

two-way price When both a bid and offer rate are quoted for a FOREX transaction.

ultra high frequency trading Trading extremely frequently; limited only by how fast you can click the mouse. Called "churning the customer's account" in the old days.

unrealized gain/loss The theoretical gain or loss on open positions valued at current market rates, as determined by the broker in its sole discretion. Unrealized gains/losses become profits/losses when the position is closed.

uptick A new price quote at a price higher than the preceding quote.

uptick rule In the United States, a regulation whereby a security may not be sold short unless the last trade prior to the short sale was at a price lower than the price at which the short sale is executed.

U.S. prime rate The interest rate at which U.S. banks will lend to their prime corporate customers.

value date The date on which counterparts to a financial transaction agree to settle their respective obligations—that is, exchange payments. For spot currency transactions, the value date is normally two business days forward. Also known as *maturity date*.

variation margin Funds a broker must request from the client to have the required margin deposited. The term usually refers to additional funds that must be deposited as a result of unfavorable price movements.

volatility   A statistical measure of a market's price movements over time characterized by deviations from a predetermined central value (usually the arithmetic mean); the gross price movement over a specified period of time given a minimum price change value. See also *directional movement* for net price movement.

whipsaw   Slang for a condition where any securities market begins moving laterally exhibiting very little volatility.

yard   Slang for a billion.

Index